SO-EAX-799

STORE PER

Norwegian-American "Paul Bunyan" of the Prairie

PETER TJERNAGEL HARSTAD

Front cover drawing, book design, and illustrations by

KARYN E. LUKASEK

With additional illustrations by Jonathan Mayer

Published in cooperation with the Evangelical Lutheran Synod Historical Society
and the Ottesen Museum, both headquartered in Mankato, Minnesota

JACKPINE PRESS • LAKEVILLE, MINNESOTA

Published by Jackpine Press
16787 Jackpine Trail
Lakeville, MN 55044-5575
ptharstad@yahoo.com

Front cover drawing, book design, and illustrations by Karyn E. Lukasek
artworkbykaryn@yahoo.com
www.mnartists.org/Karyn_Lukasek
With additional illustrations by Jonathan Mayer

Harstad, Peter Tjernagel, 1935-

Store Per: Norwegian-American "Paul Bunyan" of the Prairie

Includes maps, illustrations, appendix, bibliographical references, and index.

ISBN 978-0-615-43398-1

1. Peder Larson Tjernagel, 1826-1863 2. Norwegian-American biography and history. 3. Emigrants and emigration. 4. Frontier and pioneer life in Scott Township, Hamilton County, Iowa. 5. Lutheranism in Norway and the United States.

Printed in the United States of America by Book Printing Revolution on acid-free paper.

Dedicated to the Memory of My Mother

Martha Karina Tjernagel Harstad

Born at Follinglo Farm near Story City, Iowa, July 13, 1904, to Peder Gustav and Jennie Tjernagel, she was Store Per's grand niece. She married the Rev. Adolph M. Harstad August 12, 1931. They raised ten children of whom the author is third. When I was a lad, Mother unwittingly nudged me toward a career in history with her tales of "olden days," including versions of Store Per's feats of strength. When all of us were in school Mother worked for a decade as a cook at Bethesda Lutheran Home, Watertown, Wisconsin, where Father was Chaplain. Throughout life, Martha and Adolph enjoyed hosting visitors and, to the delight of her appreciative husband, she could "set a good table" — even with toddlers under foot. She enjoyed good health until the waning weeks of her ninety-six years and died at Tacoma, Washington, October 4, 2000.

CONTENTS

FOREWORD

Here is an engaging story about real people who participated in great events of the modern world. The mass migration of tens of millions of people from Europe to America and the transformation of the American Great Plains from virgin prairie to breadbasket of a nation and the world are compelling topics. When these broad themes are illustrated through the experience of individuals and families, they cease to be dry material one would expect to be covered in a textbook, and they come to life.

The Evangelical Lutheran Synod Historical Society and the Ottesen Museum share the goal of documenting, preserving and bringing to life for people of the twenty-first century the story of emigration of Norwegians from their homeland to the shores of America. The Synod founded the Society in 1996 to promote interest in the historical and doctrinal heritage of that branch of Lutheranism, with roots in the Norwegian Synod, which became the Evangelical Lutheran Synod of today. The Ottesen Museum bears the name of a father and a daughter. The Rev. J. A. Ottesen, one of the founders of the Norwegian Synod of 1853, fathered a history-minded daughter, Hannah, who in 1931 willed her estate (house and furnishings in Decorah, Iowa) to the Synod. The Museum contains many artifacts which belonged to the early settlers.

One of the methods by which this book relates the emigrants' story is to provide actual accounts of the lives of some of those brave souls who left their homes in Norway, crossed the wide Atlantic Ocean, and settled in the New Land called America. On the rugged, wind-swept coast of Norway, halfway between Bergen and Stavanger, the land was divided into many small farms consisting of only a few acres. The inhabitants of that coastal area could grow only a few crops and for the rest of their food they turned to the sea. Here they were able to catch fish to feed the hungry mouths of large families. Thus, between the rocky soil and the waters of Bomlo Fjord, they were able to eke out a "hand to mouth" existence.

It was here on the Lien farm that Lars Johanneson and his wife Helga lived. In the 1840s they moved to a neighboring farm called Tjernagel. They worshiped at Moster Church on Bomlo Island which they reached by boat. It is unlikely that they attended services Sunday, February 12, 1826, because that day Helga delivered her second child whom they named Peder. Thus begins the story of Peder Larson Tjernagel, who later because of his size and strength, acquired the name "Store Per" or, in English, "Big Pete." While pioneering on the prairies of Illinois and Iowa, Peder saw to it that he and the members of his family did not neglect their spiritual lives. A layman, he played a role in the founding of a Norwegian Synod congregation in Story City, Iowa. Through the twistings and turnings of history, an Evangelical Lutheran Synod congregation in Ames, Bethany Lutheran Church, traces its heritage back to the Word of God working through such sturdy pioneers as Store Per.

Store Per's story holds particular interest for me because only a few miles to the south on this same coast my father was born in 1890, and I have had the privilege of visiting Tjernagel. Father too owned an Iowa farm and that is where I grew up.

Readers with an interest in immigration history will thoroughly enjoy the story of "Big Pete" and learn much about the contributions of Norwegian immigration to this "Nation of Immigrants." But this is a book with broader appeal as well. Everyone enjoys reading about larger than life heroes. Within the covers of this book the reader will find a page-turning tale of an engaging Norwegian "Paul Bunyan of the Prairie."

George Orvick, Pastor Emeritus
Past President, Evangelical Lutheran Synod
Curator, Ottesen Museum, Mankato, Minnesota

INTRODUCTION

Growing up, I, like many of my cousins, heard Store Per stories—tales of the uncle of generations ago, named Store Per, Big Pete, somewhat resembling the Paul Bunyan of upper Midwest lore, but with the winning advantage that he was real. Our Tjernagel parents were adamant on that point.

As the generations have passed, this family of farmers, professors, teachers, craftsmen, musicians, clergymen, historians, laborers, and professional people, have spread out across the land (and the globe), have remembered some of the stories, and have maintained a curiosity about their roots. Because a few of the second generation were given to writing, recording, and saving paper and pictures, they have left a paper trail. That has made it possible for the generation presently in its sunset years to compile and examine the sources of the various lore that they heard from their parents as children. Providentially, the letters, pictures, and other memorabilia were so widely spread out, that the catastrophic December 9, 1968 plane crash at Follinglo Farm which destroyed the farmhouse and its contents, hardly dented the records of the past.

The first generation struggled to eke out an existence and build for the future. So we have little or nothing from the hands of Peder Larson Tjernagel, his brother Ole Andreas, and their cousins—Peder, Endre, and others.

But they grew a second generation who wrote, gathered, and interpreted the history. Farmer, Peder Gustav Tjernagel, wrote some of it in pencil, on a school tablet, forced to do so by his little son Alfred who knew that this *had* to be written down. Nehemias, farmer, musician, writer, and gadabout world traveler, came back to the farm after his travels, acquired a typewriter in 1912 (an Oliver, for $35.90), after which there was no stopping his literary output. Some of his writings were published as monographs, and others showed up in various periodicals. There was the brother Henry (Helge, my grandfather), the preacher in the family, who provided editing for his brothers. The oldest, Lewis (Lars Johann) had early on developed an interest in genealogy which insured that the next generations would have some records to start with.

That next generation brought more writers and even a professional historian, Neelak, a son of Henry, who acquired an Eskimo name, began the task of getting the writings of the second generation into print, done with the interest and help of others. The first publication of *The Follinglo Dog Book* came from Neelak Tjernagel's study. In the next generation came another historian with professional credentials. Peter Tjernagel Harstad was trained as a historian, taught in university history departments for a number of years and then served as director of historical societies in Iowa and Indiana. Peter has spent the years of his retirement with an indefatigable chase after various stories, one of which is the Store Per story.

Another history teacher among the descendents of the Tjernagel immigrants has remarked, originally or not, that there are only two kinds of people—those who are interested in history and those who will be. Something there was in the blood of these immigrants that led them to save papers, pictures, and stories. Something in the genes that left that rocky ledge called Tjernagel in Hordaland, Norway, was not satisfied to let the past disintegrate into the passage of time. Though there was a raw beauty to the place, it was not altogether friendly — from the air, it looks like the toes of a giant, with a little dirt oozing from between the toes. But remember they did, and after a period of oral transmission, the pencil, and then the typewriter took over.

Like Huckleberry Finn, Store Per can be read on many different levels. On the one hand, it is a boys and girls book, the story of a slightly larger than life immigrant man, who in the telling of it, has been magnified. But the story is well documented and has some sharply defined truth behind it. That, of course, is the level on which our parents told the stories to us, as they heard them from their parents, and now with another generation squeezed in.

But you don't have to have experienced the Skunk River "valley" or the Tjernagel farms northeast of Story City — the beloved "Follinglo" especially — to understand that this story reaches deeper. It provides another documentary glimpse of the process by which the prairie immigrants from the fjords and valleys of Norway mingled with immigrants from other places, including those who were here for hundreds and thousands of years before them, as well as the Yankee, older hands. Chroniclers of American life grasped early on that it was foolhardy to try to understand the American experience without paying close attention to the immigrants and their experience. The books were not at all closed after the transplanting of the Puritans, the Hudson River

Dutch, the Delaware Swedes, the Pennsylvania Germans, or the other colonizers! The shaping of the people continued with each wave of immigration, each source, and each frontier in an ever changing amalgam. Certainly, light can be shed on the immigrant experience and its contribution to the larger American culture also from what at first look seems to be familial, parochial, and regional, perhaps no less than Willa Cather does more than record the parochial story of Czech immigrants in Nebraska.

The story of Store Per portrays also a spiritual odyssey — even if not after the magnitude of Odysseus. On the one hand, we see the young Per, as a youth, certainly leaving a little bit to be desired in the exercise of responsible behavior. But he matures through his experience, so that the move to Iowa does not appear to have been born of restlessness, the desire for something different, or a better chance to strike it rich. Instead, his move involved, at least in part, a decision to provide his family with a certain type of spiritual edification, as opposed to what he sensed was the case where he found himself in Illinois.

Store Per's life was not a long one; yet along with the adventures, there was also pain and sorrow. As a common experience among the immigrants, the exceptionally high incidence of death in childhood took its toll on the outlook of the immigrants, as it did on Per. In some places it was epidemic. Per and Malena buried all of their children but one — and doubtlessly the most painful one must have been the death of little Helga who died in a prairie fire. And then came an early death for the strong Per — after digging a well in the cold of winter.

It has the makings of some real existential angst about the meaning of life, or lack thereof. But nothing of the sort suggests itself in the aftermath. Rather, Per is celebrated, and was by his own younger contemporaries, not as a sad sack who should have stayed put on the rocky Hordaland shore. In the end his contribution, as brief as it was, to the cumulative American spirit, is anything but meaningless.

Peter Tjernagel Harstad challenges one piety of received truth about the immigrant motive. Did the immigrants leave Norway (or Ireland, Germany, England) in order to find a new life and to leave behind their past? Probably so, to a greater or lesser degree. But leaving the past behind and facing only toward the new, may be an oversimplification, because, as Harstad suggests, Peder Larson Tjernagel may also have wanted to preserve something in his past. The church situation in Norway in the 1850s was chaotic. On the one hand, the Johnsonian revival led by Gisle Johnson and Carl Paul Caspari followed the Confessional revival begun in Germany thirty years before. But both rationalism and pietism, antithetical movements that they were, still had the church in Norway in unsettled turmoil. Somehow, Per's childhood religious instruction wanted something more solid than either had to offer, and if not the move to emigrate, then the move to Iowa from Illinois, seems to have more than a little to do with it. So it would appear that there is a little more complexity in the emigrant motive than often thought.

We commend this history to our kin in order to peer a little more deeply into where we have been and who we are. But we also commend it to all others who have an immigrant past, as we all do, to see another thread in the rich tapestry that brings us to what we are.

Erling T. Teigen
All Things Tjernagel www.tjernagel.org
Past Chairman, Evangelical Lutheran Synod Historical Society
Professor of Church History and Religion, Bethany Lutheran College

PROLOGUE

Every American schoolchild knows tales of Paul Bunyan and Babe, his blue ox—myths that emerged from the lumber camps of the Upper Midwest.

In contrast, few people know about Store Per, a flesh and blood strongman who grew up in Norway, and then left for America with little more than his bride, his Bible, and his violin. After an encounter with the pinewood forests of Wisconsin, the young couple found their bearings in the New World while living among fellow Norwegians in Wisconsin and Illinois, then crossed the Mississippi to wrest a farm from the virgin prairie of central Iowa. Per toiled with his oxen, made music with his violin, and experienced joy as well as excruciating sorrow. At times, his temper flared. He knew that he fell short of God's standards but he did not despair. Wherever he went his optimism, feats of strength, competence, and good humor raised people's spirits.

Like the Paul Bunyan tales, the Store Per stories passed through the lens of Scandinavian exaggeration. Nevertheless, at the core of the stories is a real person with aspirations and faults, hopes and dreams, who lived, loved, toiled, believed, and died.

Was he just another frontiersman, or, in the language of his native land, *enestaende*, unique and in a class by himself? The pages that follow challenge the reader to decide.

Chapter One
BIRTH AND HERITAGE

Childbirth is like standing a piece of flatbread on edge;
you never know which way it will fall [toward life or death].

The days are bleak and short on Norway's west coast during the early weeks of the year; the nights interminable. Fishermen have good reasons for staying in port. It is too early in the season for netting herring and too dark and dangerous to venture out on rough seas for a catch of mackerel. Farmers tend their animals but there is nothing to do in the fields. When the north wind howls the place to be is at home beside the hearth.

In early February 1826, twenty-eight year old Lars Johanneson, a farmer and fisherman who lived on Bomlo Fjord near the sixtieth parallel, had an additional reason for staying home. His wife, Helga Pedersdatter, was counting days until the birth of her second child. At age twenty-five she already had a two-year old son, Johannes.

Norwegian farms have names. The couple lived on the Lien farm in Sveen parish. Now known as Sveio, it is in the county of Hordaland, midway between Bergen to the north and Stavanger to the south. A generation earlier this nine-acre farm fronting Bomlo Fjord supported one family. Lars leased half of it, less than two acres of which are arable. At a latitude nearly identical to that of Skagway, Alaska, Lars and Helga grew small grains and potatoes. The nights are too cool and the growing season

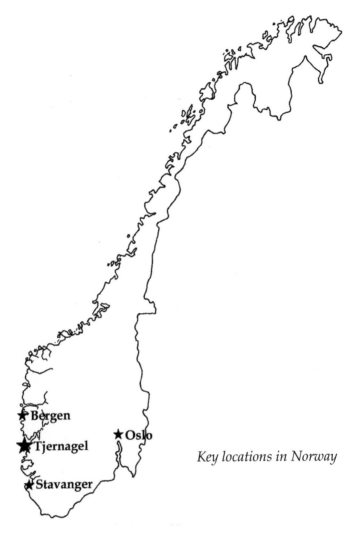

Key locations in Norway

is too short for growing corn (maize). Portions of the farm not under cultivation were suitable only for pasture and hay.

No trees of any size grow on or near the Lien farm but peat deposits supplied fuel for cooking and warmth. Lars took what he needed according to established rules. He cut into the peat with a special spade and used a three-tined wooden fork to remove blocks of uniform size. When dried, the peat burned slowly in stoves and hearths. It generated ample heat and also prodigious quantities of smoke.

Helga's older sister Kjersteen Pedersdatter lived on the other half of the Lien farm with her husband Phillipus Knutson and their children. Each family had its own home and outbuildings. Because their fields were small and rocky, they relied upon the sea for a portion of their diet and livelihood. Their situation was not unusual. Many Norwegian families lived on small *gards* and eked out a living as best they could.

Adjoining the Lien farm on the west is the Tjernagel (pronounced *chair-nah-gull*) North farm with its main buildings near the water. Next to it, with its buildings on higher ground, is the Tjernagel South farm. For generations Lars and Helga's forebears had lived on or near these farms. The two sisters had grown up at Tjernagel South in better circumstances than they now experienced. Nevertheless, they were thankful for being better off than those who worked for others and owned or leased no property. In northern Europe such people were known as cotters.

On Sunday, February 12, 1826, Helga went into labor and called for her sister, Kjersteen, an experienced birth helper or *hjelpekone*. The news spread and women arrived from surrounding farms to lend assistance. One of their tasks was to supplement the peat fuel in the hearth with juniper branches. According to a widely held belief, the snapping and crackling of burning juniper protected the mother and child from *huldrefolk* (hidden people) who might cause harm. Common people then saw no conflict between their folkways and their Christian faith.

Delivery of a male child exhausted Helga and taxed Kjersteen's midwifery skills to the limit. Then, when the pulse in the umbilical cord weakened, the experienced *hjelpekone* tied it off in two places and cut the cord at a right angle between the ties. It was thought that a diagonal cut could cause developmental defects in the baby. Even today when a Norwegian makes a mistake or asks a foolish question, a jesting friend might ask: "Wasn't your umbilical cord cut right?" Following custom, Norwegian mothers squirted breast milk into the eyes of their newborns to prevent blindness.

After attending to such matters it became apparent that the baby was not doing well. In fact, his life was so precarious that immediate baptism was in order. The parish church and pastor were on the opposite shore of Bomlo Fjord. Therefore, the parents summoned a respected layman, Jon Omundsen, from the neighboring Oklandsnes farm. He promptly administered the sacrament and bestowed upon Peder Larson his first name. Ironic it is that life began precariously for the future strongman.

In days to come when neighbors visited Helga they noticed that her baby was gaining strength. The next documented fact about Peder is that on March 4, 1826, his parents took him by boat across Bomlo Fjord to *Moster Kirke* for the affirmation of his christening. Vicar Christian Hertzberg recorded the event in the Finnas Parish *kirkebok*, along with a full contingent of sponsors, including his helpful aunt, Kjersteen. This capable woman and members of her family appear frequently in Peder's life from beginning to end.

Moster Church where Helga and Lars brought Peder is one of the oldest Christian churches in Norway. In an ancient Norse saga, Snorre Sturlason (1178-1241) relates how Olav Trygvason crossed the North Sea from England and came to Moster in 995 to become king of Norway. He pitched his tent, celebrated mass, and built a church. At this site stands an upright stone with a slit near the top. For centuries people of the locality related that King Olav kicked this spot to make a hitching post so that he could tie up his horse. They detected the imprint of the royal instep on one side of the stone "and the place where the battered toes went through on the other." An 1892 American visitor to these environs reported remnants of such ancient superstitions "clinging to the moss in the old log walls of many a backwoods hut." Visitors to the churchyard in July 2010 received instructions for renewing their marriage vows while shaking hands through the slit in this ancient rock.

During the Viking era this portion of coast constituted the dynamic center of Norway because of its timber stands, fisheries, and accessibility. Diminutive Moster Church stands on the Trygvason site near a substantial deposit of lime, an essential ingredient of mortar and plaster. Constructed in the twelfth century with hewn stone and later given a slate roof, the building has weathered the centuries remarkably well. When workmen removed plaster from the south wall in 1947 they found a runic inscription imploring almighty God "to take care of N. N. Ragnarsson who carved these runes." As of 2010 a coat of fresh plaster covered the exterior of the church.

Since the Middle Ages two bells in the loft have pealed out over land and water to summon worshipers, "the smaller one cast with a representation of St. Olav and the inscription 'Ave Maria gratia plena. Dominus tecum.'"

(Hail, Mary, full of Grace. The Lord is with you.) The Roman Catholic Church acquired large tracts of land in this vicinity and received payments from the peasants who farmed them, including Peder's forebears.

After the teachings of the Lutheran Reformation took hold in northern Germany and were codified in the Augsburg Confession of 1530, they spread to Scandinavia. King Christian III of Denmark, whose rule extended over Norway, declared Norway Lutheran in 1537. Clergymen who did not answer to Rome and who exercised their Christian freedom by taking wives, taught that salvation from sin and death comes to fallen mankind by the grace of God alone, through the life, death, and resurrection of the incarnate Son of God. Further, that salvation is given to human beings through the Means of Grace, the Gospel in Word and Sacraments, Baptism and the Lord's Supper. Faith alone, which only God can give, enables individuals to embrace it.

Centuries-old political considerations determined forms of worship to support Lutheran theology. As of 1397 Denmark, Sweden, and Norway were united under the Kalmar union, but in 1536 Denmark relegated Norway to the status of a province. When Martin Luther's pastor and confessor Johannes Bugenhagen (1485-1558) wrote an order of service for the Lutheran church in Denmark, it came into use in Norway as well. The Bugenhagen liturgy set up a doctrinally and musically rich dialogue between the officiant and the congregation. Peder learned it as a boy at Moster Church.

A hallmark of Lutheran teaching is the way it answers a basic question: Do good deeds make a good person and give salvation, or does a person who has salvation by the grace of God alone produce good deeds as the fruits of faith? On the basis of Scripture, Lutheranism's answer was the latter. Rationalism of the eighteenth-century Enlightenment worked to undermine this doctrine, but it survived for Peder and many others in the Lutheran Church of Norway through their hearing of the Gospel in Word and Sacrament. As an adult far removed from his birthplace, Peder would go to great lengths to ensure that he and his family worshiped in congregations with pastors faithful to the Christian creeds and the Lutheran confessions. The spirit of the Reformation brought renovations to the interior of Moster Church. To facilitate the dissemination of the Gospel, a pulpit was installed in the chancel and oak pews in the nave. During Peder's youth these same high-backed pews, "hard as stone," prevented little eyes from wandering from the pastor in the raised pulpit to friends seated with their parents, males to the right of the center aisle, females and infants to its left. If not from the pulpit, then at the communion rail the pastor detected the aroma of fishing boats and cattle barns clinging to the homespun clothing of his parishioners.

While people mingled after Sunday services Peder played in the churchyard with a shy lad of his own age, Lars Henderson, whose family lived at Oiro at the base of Mount Siggen (Siggjo on modern maps) in the northern reaches of the parish. One can imagine the boys playing on a limestone block, once part of a pillory where offenders were publicly shamed. Someone called Peder's little playmate *Taalige* Lars, meaning patient or quiet, and intended as a term of endearment. The label stuck, and that is how Peder knew him during a friendship that lasted not only from Sunday to Sunday but throughout life. Peder too received a descriptive sobriquet (to be explained shortly). At crucial times during their lives Peder and Lars were inseparable and made important decisions together.

Sveen, where Peder spent his formative years, means "burned over" and was anything but prosperous. Nevertheless, his generation saw the century-old baptismal font at Moster Church come into frequent use. It carries an inscription explaining that the crew of the East Indiaman, *Queen Anna Sophia*, donated the basin "in gratitude for their vessel's escape from danger and safe anchorage in Moster harbour at the turn of the year 1721/1722." A North Sea storm had struck terror even into seasoned sailors who had rounded the Cape of Good Hope and traversed the Indian Ocean. Some, if not all of Peder's siblings received the Sacrament of Holy Baptism at this font.

Simultaneously with a nationwide increase in birth rate came improvements in nutrition and public health. Early in the nineteenth century *potet prester* (potato pastors) encouraged the people of their parishes to plant this nourishing New World crop. The Norwegian government also instructed clergymen to follow the lead of Dr. Edward Jenner in England and vaccinate their parishioners against smallpox. Consistent with Enlightenment goals of using human intelligence to improve the lot of mankind, such duties, nonetheless, came with a downside. They transformed pastors into government agents increasingly occupied with the "here and now" and diminished their roles as spiritual leaders. Pietistic lay preachers filled the void but created other problems. Pietism "leads to a selfish satisfaction with one's own penitence," concluded a Swedish bishop, "and a merciless judgment of the children of the world." As an adult Peder rejected pietism. This affected the course of his life, as related in Chapter Six.

Norway's population of 883,487 in 1801 increased to 1,490,047 in 1855. A near doubling of the population squeezed many west coast families into poverty on farms of only a few acres. These people were not isolated. They learned about the world from Norwegian sailors who traveled widely as well as from seamen of other nations who visited their ports.

In 1814 diplomats from Europe's major powers assembled in Vienna to make peace after the ravages of the Napoleonic Wars. Their decisions changed the lives even of the common people of Norway. Victors penalized defeated nations by the loss of territory. Thus Denmark lost Norway to the Swedish Crown. Influenced by Enlightenment thinking, Norway's leaders insisted on having their own constitution, a parliament, and greater freedom. On May 17, 1814, a constitution with such provisions became reality but independence from Sweden would have to wait until 1905.

Nevertheless, a distinctive national consciousness was born and *Syttende Mai* (May 17) became Norway's national holiday. One of the freedoms Norwegians gained under the Swedish Crown was the right to leave the country. This set the stage for the beginnings of Norwegian immigration to America in 1825. The century that followed witnessed an exodus of epic proportions of which Store Per was a part. Only Ireland with its potato famines and displaced cotters provided the United States with as many immigrants in proportion to its population.

Moster Church

Peder was the second of eight children born to Helga and Lars, all, with one possible exception, delivered by Kjersteen. Tradition decreed that the firstborn son be named after his paternal grandfather and the second after his maternal grandfather. Thus, Lars and Helga named their first son Johannes and the second Peder. Following the same convention, Kjersteen and Phillipus named their second son Peder after the same man.

The family fortune reached its zenith in the Old Country in the person of *"Peder Andersson Tjernagel, sore"* (1768-1814), father of Helga, Kjersteen, and five others. His property, sub-farm # 3 at Tjernagel South, supported a horse, seven cattle, thirteen sheep, and four goats. An

13

energetic and capable man, he diversified his endeavors. In addition to farming, he learned the blacksmith's trade, bought tools for his workshop, and acquired a share in a herring sweep net. The people of Tjernagel regarded him as "very well off." However, he "drowned in the ice" Christmas Eve 1814 at age forty-six. As Peder's children matured circumstances forced them onto smaller farms and they had to make-do with fewer resources than they enjoyed as part of their father's household early in the century.

Peder's daughters, Kjersteen and Helga, illustrate this point. After they married and settled down on the subdivided Lien farm, they and their growing families struggled to make a living. Kjersteen's husband, Phillipus, bought parcel # 1 of the Lien farm in 1820. Helga's husband Lars leased parcel # 2 in 1823. Meadowland provided pasture for a few head of livestock and for making hay, but each family had less than two acres for growing crops. Insufficient land, not lack of industry, thwarted their efforts. With the increase in birth and survival rates, there was not enough farmland in Norway to support its population.

Names carried more meaning in Norway during the 1800s than they do in most parts of the world today. Peder, a common name among west coast fishing families, is the Norwegian form of Peter, after the Galilean fisherman commissioned by Christ himself to be a fisher of men. For the second sons of Helga and Kjersteen the name also indicated a once prosperous maternal lineage. Given the conventions of the time and place, "Larson" was inevitable for the future strongman, indicating that this Peder was the son of Lars.

How and why Tjernagel, bordering both the Lien farm and a small cove on Bomlo Fjord, became part of Peder's full name requires explanation. For generations, people on both sides of his family owned portions of either the Tjernagel North or Tjernagel South farms. During Peder's youth several families lived on these farms. Some of them owned land, others leased or rented land, and still others lived as workers and landless cotters.

As Lars' family grew and an older generation died off, he continued farming at Lien until 1854 and expanded his operation into "share no. 2" of the Tjernagel North farm. Lars moved his family into a more spacious house there in the early 1840s and bought the share in 1847, subject to the terms of a waning feudal land system. Because of repeated parceling of the farm it is difficult to determine how many acres he acquired, but it was more than he leased at Lien. Moreover, the land was "good for grain production."

For generations the family had been making such moves among *klostergods,* farms that had once belonged to Lyse Monastery of the Cistercian order founded at Os, Hordaland, in 1146. The founding abbot came from near York in England, but the order was French whose monks were known for introducing useful plants such as fruit trees. Cistercian monasteries "on a rather regular basis developed into big landowners with a broad range of businesses." At the time of the Reformation the Danish crown confiscated the monastery's vast holdings and the king's feudal lords collected rents previously paid to the Roman Catholic Church.

Under the constitution of May 17, 1814, the Norwegian government collected the rents and allocated the income to religious and educational purposes. As long as Lars lived he paid these obligations, reckoned in quantities of butter and animal skins. The last of these obligations was extinguished at Tjernagel North in 1894, whereupon the holders of the property finally owned their land outright. Foundation stones and a few upright columns of Lyse Monastery near the southern outskirts of Bergen are reminders of an early chapter of Norway's deep past.

Norwegians became increasingly mobile as the 1800s progressed, but they continued to use a small pool of first names. Country people who moved to cities as well as those who crossed the Atlantic frequently encountered others of the very same name. Peder Larson was a very common name. Using the place he came from as part of his name clarified this Peder Larson's identity. Well into the twentieth century his nephews referred to him as "Peder Larson Tjernagel" — Peder, son of Lars, who hailed from Tjernagel. In some documents his name appears as Peder Larson Lien after the farm where he was born.

Per or *Peer* (pronounced *pear*) is the Norwegian abbreviation for Peder, comparable to Pete for Peter in English. Following his precarious start in life the boy flourished. Neighbors, kin, and people at church called him "Store Per," Big Pete. They rolled the "r" in their word for big (large, great) and they pronounced a final short "e" —*store*. In time the nickname crossed the Atlantic with him. Therefore, readers may pronounce *store* or *stor* either in the Norwegian way or just as it appears in English.

The name "Per" or"*Peer*" is known throughout the world because two Norwegian artists, playwright Henrik Ibsen and composer Edvard Grieg, combined talents to create an unforgettable character of this name with words and music. Their Peer is anything but heroic. A "lazy, lying, philandering lout," he travels the world and becomes rich on money made through slavery. Peer Gynt learns nothing as he matures, only to be redeemed at last by the love of beautiful and faithful Solveig. Readers might look for "Peer Gynt moments" in the life of Store Per.

Layers of history go into the making of human beings. This book presents known facts about Store Per, fits him into successive settings where he lived, and records stories and legends that grew up around the man. Readers are forewarned that some informants stretched reality.

Conscientious parents, Christianity, traditions rooted in the farms and fishing villages of Hordaland, schooling, life at sea, and numerous challenges honed Per's character and shaped his destiny. Although he did not always live up to them, the values he received as a lad had consequences decades later on another continent. The mature Store Per would be the first to acknowledge the role of a loving and forgiving God in his life.

A *stor* person in every sense of the word, Store Per developed a unique, multifaceted, and pleasing personality that enabled him to cut through barriers and turn rivals into friends. Many Store Per tales elaborate deeds that he performed to live up to his name and reputation. They grew in the telling to the point that, in the minds of some Norwegian-Americans, he became a larger-than-life "Paul Bunyan" of the prairie. To be confident in their New World setting these people needed heroes, so they created their own.

Does Peder Larson Tjernagel (1826-1863), the real person at the core of the Store Per stories, merit the designation "hero?" Following is evidence to consider while deciding.

Chapter Two

AN OLD COUNTRY YOUTH

Den skal tidlig krokes, som god krok skal bli.
To become a good hook, you should be bent early.

Other than vital statistics, few details from Store Per's early years survive. He grew up in a household consisting of his parents, an older brother, Johannes, and six younger siblings: Gunhild, Helga, Ole Andreas (who died as an infant), a second Ole Andreas (a maternal great grandfather of this writer), Barbru, and Larsine. During his youth Per interacted frequently with aunts, uncles, and cousins at Lien and the two Tjernagel farms. Closest in physical proximity were Kjersteen, her husband Phillipus, and their seven children, four of whom reached adulthood: Helga, Anna Marie, Knut, and Peder. Later, when this family came to America the younger generation took the name Phillops. Per had numerous playmates but early death claimed one of his siblings and three of Kjersteen's children, his first cousins.

Wooden boats constituted the standard mode of transportation in the fjord country. Regardless of size or means of propulsion (oars or sails), the design of these keeled vessels was basically that of the Viking long boats. However, the prows and sterns did not sweep up as abruptly as did those of the sleek warships of a thousand years earlier. At Lien, Lars and Phillipus could beach small boats on their own property. The same was true at

19

Tjernagel North where it was also possible to dock ships in protected water.

Store Per grew up on the water with his father as mentor for learning about the sea. On Sundays, Lars used his fishing boat to transport the family across the fjord to attend services at Moster Church. Bigger and more substantial vessels with strong masts, large sails, and ample holds were necessary for cod fishing in the far north.

This is how Iowa-born Nehemias Tjernagel, son of Ole Andreas and nephew of Store Per, described the family home on the fjord at Tjernagel North when he visited there in July 1892. Little had changed since the early 1840s when the family moved there from Lien.

> . . . the house was rather low, with the rooms, both upstairs and downstairs, to correspond. The windows were few enough, and . . . the living room was less cheerful than it would have been if the sun could have peeped in from the south. A small kitchen and a corner to store fuel — peat mostly — occupied one end of the building, and from here an ancient oven was run through the wall into the dining and sitting room, answering the purpose of a cook stove at one end and a heating stove at the other. It emitted considerable smoke from the slow-burning peat, but otherwise answered its purpose very well, considering its age, which was two centuries.

Looking out the window to the north that clear summer day Nehemias saw Mount Siggjo rising majestically from Moster Island. Distances across the water deceived the Iowan. The opposite shore seemed "scarcely more than a mile distant," Nehemias wrote home, "while in reality it is 7 miles away." To the northeast stood snow-clad

mountains. To the east lay Folgefonna Glacier producing icy blue water for the fjord. To the west "The water is as smooth as glass at this moment," explained Nehemias, "and the setting sun, saying goodbye between the hills, reflects a golden highway across the fjord." On such days, Tjernagel constituted a place of beauty that one could hardly imagine leaving.

Making a living in this setting was another matter. Were it not for the sea, Lars could not have provided sufficient food for his family. By Iowa standards, the fields on the Lien and Tjernagel farms are small and the soil is rocky. The earliest reference to a potato crop at Tjernagel North appears in an agricultural report of 1802. The next available report, that of 1866, indicates harvests of sixty-two Norwegian *tonne* of potatoes and 104 of oats. (A *tonne* is 19.9 liters larger than a three-bushel American barrel.) Several families inhabiting the farm subsisted on these quantities.

When Nehemias returned to Tjernagel in 1910 after years of tilling Iowa's rich soil, he wrote his brother and farming partner, Peder Gustav: "Tjernagel itself and the land . . . in its vicinity has much of stone and heather and does not give off much of growth either wild or cultivated." Yet, with frequent applications of seaweed and animal manure "the little areas broken for cultivation produce fairly well." Norwegian relatives found Nehemias hard to believe when he reported yields in excess of a hundredfold for kernels of corn planted in the American heartland—a crop that does not mature at the latitude of Tjernagel.

South of Tjernagel the coastline turns bleak and the land is less productive because few inlets and no offshore islands offer protection from North Sea winds and weather. Moreover, the currents of the Hardanger Fjord here meet the open sea, complicating navigation. *Sletten,* the area is called. Nehemias learned, first hand, that the term is "synonymous with seasickness." Nautical considerations tended to orient the Tjernagels northward toward Bergen rather than southward toward Hauge-sund and Stavanger.

Fish caught in Bomlo Fjord and marketed in Bergen assured that the inhabitants of Tjernagel would have a little money for buying necessities. Commercial fishing, especially the netting of herring, was carefully regulated. The right to fish in some places was attached to ownership of the adjacent property; in other locations fishing and netting rights were inherited, bought, and

AN OLD COUNTRY YOUTH

sold. Nature bestowed her bounties, but one had to follow prescribed rules for catching fish and even for mining peat.

The Larson Tjernagels consumed what their acres produced. They planted, harvested, flailed, and winnowed oats, barley, wheat, and rye in much the same way that people performed these tasks in Biblical times. A gristmill operated at Tjernagel North when a stream that emptied into the fjord had sufficient flow to turn the grinding stones. A typical errand for young Store Per was to take grain to the mill and wait while the miller ground it into the consistency ordered by his mother.

Cutting hay with sickles, curing it on fence-like structures, and storing it in the barn for the long winter months engaged all members of the family. The number of animals that could be kept over winter depended upon the hay supply. Large beasts such as horses and cattle consumed large amounts of fodder, so their number must be limited. Sheep and goats consumed less and were useful for wool and milk. Small farms supported only one hog. It would be butchered at the onset of winter and replaced in the spring when the piglet peddler from Etne made his rounds. "These pigs are fourteen days going on the third week" was his annual pitch, "and eat just exactly anything they get, sir." Store Per took his turn at feeding herring heads to the family pig.

In 1802 the two Tjernagel farms supported a total of two horses, nineteen cattle, and two dozen sheep. Animal counts went up in subsequent decades, but not in proportion to the increase in population. If a household the size of Lars and Helga's (nine people in the 1840s) owned two cows, ten sheep, and a goat or two they were deemed well off. Children wore "homespun" made from wool that family members sheared, carded, spun into yarn, and knitted into clothing. For these and other household tasks Helga enlisted the services of her four daughters as soon as they were old enough to help. An elderly relative testified to Nehemias that she had "never since childhood worn a stitch of clothing save what she had knitted or spun herself." Store Per and his siblings could name the sheep whose fibers kept them warm.

Making items out of wood kept the males busy during winter months. Leather shoes for fast-growing children were beyond the reach of most families. Therefore, the fathers used special tools to carve wooden shoes. Store Per learned this craft from his father, Lars. Tools that they used exist to this day. There is an old saying that wooden shoes are symbols of peace. Whoever heard of a thief or villain on the prowl in noisy wooden shoes?

Children slept in narrow beds, *himmelseng*, boarded in to keep them from tumbling out and to contain warm quilts when the north wind howled. Some contend that nestling into these snug environments gave Norwegian children a sense of security that helped them weather the storms of life. As he grew, Store Per developed self-confidence that enabled him to step out into the world and cope with difficulties.

Furniture and kitchenware were also of wood. In the living room *kubbestoler* hewn from vertical logs and decorated with carvings provided seating for adults. Children used benches of appropriate height. Wooden bowls, plates, and utensils served everyday use. When Nehemias visited Tjernagel in 1892 he sat at the very table where Store Per and his siblings bowed their heads in prayer, ate with wooden spoons, and laughed fifty years earlier. In those bygone times Helga brought her treasured glass and china pieces out of the cupboard only on special occasions.

Products from the farm and sea became nutritious food in Helga's kitchen. Some red meat was available, particularly in the early winter. Fish could be caught throughout the year, but fishing could be dangerous in the winter months. According to family tradition, a fish should be so fresh that it lives "to see its own frying-pan." Apple trees thrive on Norway's west coast as do pear and cherry trees and a variety of berries.

From oats, barley, and rye grown on the farm and then ground to various consistencies at the local mill, came gruel for porridge (*grot*) and flour for a variety of uses. Helga frequently made oatcakes and batches of a thin, crisp, unleavened flatbread (*flatbrod*) that she baked in her peat-burning stove. Universally liked, flatbread traveled well on fishing voyages and other ventures away from home. From rye flour Helga made nourishing bread. It too traveled and kept well. As in Ireland, potatoes constituted a dietary mainstay. If a potato crop failed, cotters a notch or two below the Larsons in the stratified society of the day faced starvation.

Lefse, made of flour, milk, and water, was rolled flat to about a foot and a half in diameter, and then baked on top of the stove. Spread with butter, sprinkled with sugar, and rolled into cylindrical form, it was a special treat. Dairy products came to the table in many forms ranging from fresh milk and butter to cheese and desserts. At Christmastime the latter took the form of *rommegrot* topped with cinnamon from the East Indies and sugar from the West Indies, luxuries purchased in Bergen with money from the sale of fish. No evidence suggests that lack of nutrition stunted Store Per's growth.

During the coldest months of the year even the water of Bomlo Fjord freezes. Among the pleasures of Norwegian children were ice-skating, skiing, and sledding in wintertime, and, in the warm months, boating, and hiking up into the higher elevations. There waterfalls leap and sparkle in the sunlight and make rainbows in the spray. Salted herring, flatbread, and *gjetost*, a sweet brown cheese made from goats' milk, made tasty lunches for extended outings. Packing such items into a decorated wooden lunch box whose lid doubled as a cutting board was part of the ritual.

In spring, colorful wildflowers carpet the mountain meadows called *saeters* and present incomparable beauty. Some farm families possessed grazing rights in these summer pastures to which they herded their cattle, sheep, and goats. Thus, even the animals went on vacation after long winter confinements. Girls tended the flocks and made butter and cheese from the milk of cows, goats, and even sheep under their care. Life was pleasant in the mountain huts during long summer days when sunset slipped imperceptibly into dawn.

Young males helped their fathers with heavy farm work and fishing tasks such as netting herring in the fjords. Enormous schools of herring came to Norway's west coast in the spring and were a source of income at Tjernagel. After the herring swam back to sea the young men visited their sisters and other girls in the high country. In these idyllic settings romance frequently kindled between flaxen-haired *saeter* beauties and their swain. When the days shortened and cool weather returned, the girls drove the flocks home, lengthy cod and mackerel fishing expeditions ceased, and families reunited.

Nature waited until then to put on her most spectacular show. As Nehemias gazed heavenward from Tjernagel one night in 1892, "Arms of white flame (Aurora Borealis) shot up from the horizon on the north and stretched toward us till they reached after us both above and beyond." The Iowan wrote home: "I was almost afraid I might be snatched up and lifted into illimitable space. God's handiwork, indeed."

What later generations termed myths touched everyday life in the years of Store Per's youth. Following thought patterns of their Viking forebears, people assigned human attributes to features of the natural environment. Thus giants (*jotul*) lived in vast rooms in the mountains and furnished inspiration for such artists as Edvard Grieg. Valkyries, maidens of Odin, caused storms and Neptune determined the fate of ships on the North Sea. Other beings inhabited forests and eddies in streams. Each had its name and personality. Stunted trolls with frightfully ugly faces frequented rocky places beneath bridges. But, through the mists, mosses, and mysterious shadows, humans caught only fleeting glimpses of these ethereal creatures.

With camera in hand and tongue in cheek, Store Per's nephew, Nehemias, once stalked Norway's shadow people but failed utterly in attempts to photograph any of them.

Evidence of pre-Christian thought still lingers in Norway and the western world. Wednesday (Woden's Day, *onsdag*) received its name from Wuotan or Odin, chief of the Norse gods who demonstrated his genius by inventing runes (letters); Thursday (*torsdag*) from Thor who threw his hammer in the heavens and drove his chariot over mountaintops to produce thunder and lightning. Friday (*fredag*) from Frigg, goddess of love. To this day Friday is a favored day of the week for courting.

A wealth of stories and myths surround Norwegian place names. According to one researcher, *Tjernagel* stems from Old Norse *Hiarnagli* meaning sword rivet. Store Per heard other, and perhaps more credible explanations. *Tjer* (or *tjaer*) is the Norwegian word for tar; *nagel* the Germanic word for nail. One explanation of "tar nail" is that, in days of yore, boat builders at Tjernagel constructed superior craft by dipping their nails in tar so that they would not rust and loosen.

An alternate explanation is more complex. Rock lining the small cove at Tjernagel drops precipitously into deep water. Therefore, ships can safely tie up to mooring spikes driven into the rock. From Viking times the cove served as a trading place as well as a haven for ships tormented by squalls. Seamen circled the spikes with tar so they could see them from a distance. Hence the name Tjernagel (tar nail).

Survival at this latitude depends upon people's ability to predict storms, determine their bearings at sea and in the mountains, understand currents and tides, and to read nature's clock. Lars and Helga had no clocks or watches, but they taught their children to tell time by the sun and the shadows it casts. While learning to observe seasonal change at age ten, Store Per's younger brother Ole Andreas carved a figure into a wall of the family home at Tjernagel North "to show how high the sun went" throughout the year. Nehemias found his father's boyhood carving undisturbed when he visited Norway in 1892 and included a rough sketch of it in a letter he mailed home July 16.

When shown to astronomer Susan Lederer of California State University at San Bernardino early in 2007, she immediately identified the sketch as an analemma, a diagram plotting the high point of the sun in the sky during the course of a year as viewed from a fixed location, in this case the Tjernagel home. If plotted accurately, such diagrams take the shape of a figure 8. Perhaps the ancient Norse blended mythology with science when they pictured Odin's horse Gleipnir with eight legs. From Viking times tables existed for showing the sun's midday high point for each week at specific latitudes. With such a table in hand a navigator could measure the noontime angle between the sun and the horizon and get a fair estimate of his ship's latitude.

Lars had practical reasons for teaching his children to observe the heavenly bodies. From them they could approximate the time of day, direction, and latitude. Understanding the winds, currents, and tides would require time and experience. Store Per learned to row, sail, and navigate at an early age. Venturing beyond the cove, into the fjord, and returning home constituted steps toward independence. Developing the skills to sail to Bomlo Island in the fog and return home safely would come in time. Most important was the development of judgment about when to stay in port, areas to avoid, and what to do in emergencies.

Children learned about the sea and about life when accompanying their elders as they went about their business. A youthful Ole Andreas heard this threat from a fishmonger at Bergen: "I will give you a black eye with a yellow shutter if you don't look out." With a ten year head start in life Store Per mentored his younger brother about how to handle himself at sea and around such toughs. An all too frequent close to biographies of Norwegian fishermen is *"fall over bord og drukna* (drowned)." The sea is dangerous, but Store Per and Ole Andreas returned home safely from all of their fishing trips and youthful adventures. Their older brother Johannes did not. His fate, to the extent that it can be determined, is related in the next chapter.

In addition to learning by being part of the Lien and Tjernagel communities, young Store Per attended school during the winter months. The state provided professional schoolmasters, usually stern males who dressed formally in vests and knee-breeches and brooked no nonsense in their classes, often held in people's homes. Church and state were not separate and religion was part of the curriculum. A bright, fun-loving lad with a dimpled chin, Store Per achieved competence in "the common branches of knowledge." One source relates that while he was a schoolboy Per read blood-curdling stories about American Indians.

A right of passage for a Norwegian boy came when his parents decided that he was responsible enough to own his own knife. It would be useful while fishing and also enable him to whittle and carve alongside the older males. A knife and a homemade leather scabbard might come as Christmas gifts.

Whittling, loafing, dreaming, hiking, rowing, sailing, working, skiing, ice-skating and gaining strength were part of Store Per's youth. Active outdoor life on land and sea made his cheeks red and his muscles strong. An "ever shifting panorama on the fjord with its changing hues, the passing ships, the swooping sea-gulls, squalls, white-caps, and more" signaled that life too would be fraught with change. Per understood the small sailboats, zigzagging toward their destinations. Watching large ships cruise by piqued his imagination about the world beyond Norway.

Store Per observed that life tossed some people about while others, including his father, plied a steady course. No records survive to indicate the profitability of Lars' fishing operations, but there is no question about his ability as a farmer. As a young man Lars made the most of the meager resources of the Lien farm and then bought larger and better fields on the Tjernagel North farm. These as well as his grazing land, Lars put to good use. A good provider for his family, he was also a worthy role model for his children.

Helga and Lars took seriously the spiritual needs of their children. The family said grace before and after meals, sang the melodic hymns of Scandinavian and German hymnodists, held devotions, and worshiped at the parish church of the Evangelical Lutheran Church of Norway (the state church) to which they were assigned. For most, if not all of the time that they lived at Lien, this was the ancient Moster Church in Finnas Parish, across the fjord on Bomlo Island. Prior to 1852, Finnas and Sveio Parishes operated as a unit and clergymen often served more than one church. Records do not always indicate which church in the two parishes a family attended. According to the Reverend Kolbein Espeset who served at Sveio, "There is not, and has never been, a parish church at Lien or Tjernagel." Attending church involved Sunday morning trips of seven miles each way, regardless of whether the Larsons of Tjernagel boated across the fjord to Moster Church or walked to church at the village of Sveio.

At age fourteen or fifteen, Norwegian children reached a milestone in life. Following a course of study centering on Dr. Martin Luther's *Small Catechism* and Bishop Erik Pontoppidan's *Explanation of the Catechism*, the pastor examined them. All would have to recite and comprehend key Bible verses such as Ephesians 2:8-9: "For it is by grace you have been saved, through faith— and this not from yourselves, it is the gift of God—not by works, so that no one can boast."

When they met the pastor's standards the students were "confirmed" in the Christian faith and became eligible to receive the Sacrament of Holy Communion. For many, confirmation marked the end of formal schooling. The Finnas Parish *kirkebok* shows that Peder was confirmed November 14, 1841, with the mark "Very good." In daily life confirmands were no longer to be considered children but young women and men with a degree of independence. Throughout life, Store Per remained faithful to the church of his youth.

Two of Store Per's first cousins who grew up on the Tjernagel South farm took to the sea shortly after they were confirmed. It would not be long before Per would follow suit.

Chapter Three
BECOMING AN ADULT

The music of every country starts with folk songs.

Among the certain facts about Store Per is that he matured in a family that loved music. He learned that music, in its many moods and manifestations, can turn the current of people's lives. During the middle decades of the nineteenth century an ornate style of singing "with trills and quavers and semi-quavers and crescendos and diminuendos without end" remained in vogue in Norway. At home, adults bounced children on their knees while singing spirited lays (*bygde viser*) in this style. At church, people wove harmonious variations into congregational singing so skillfully "that the melody itself was not lost but rather enhanced by this tuneful by-play." Harmonious embellishments came easily for Store Per and carried over from singing to another area of his musicianship. He became a competent violinist with a special interest in the folk melodies of his own locality.

A great violinist and native of Bergen, Ole Bull (1809-1880), set high standards for Norwegians who took to that instrument. Seventeen years older than Store Per, Bull "blended classical standards with melodies he had learned as a youth—somber ancient ballads, bold dance tunes, melancholy herding and love songs, religious standards and simple folk ditties." Virtuoso playing coupled with an engaging but eccentric personality made Bull a wealthy international celebrity even as a young man. Americans lionized him during a concert tour that began in 1843 and lasted through 1845.

Largely through Bull's influence, Norwegians developed pride in the music of their country, especially when played on the Hardanger fiddle (*hardingfele*). This heavily ornamented instrument differs from the conventional violin in that it has two sets of strings. Four strings on a conventional fingerboard are usually tuned in the same way as the violin, from bottom to top G, D, A, and E. A second set of four or five strings under the fingerboard vibrates "sympathetically," resulting in a droning echo reminiscent of Scottish bagpipe music.

One of Bull's friends wrote: "Most people knew the folk-songs and dances, but were ashamed to admire them." Under Bull's influence, "homely melodies suddenly began to gleam like stars, and the people came to feel that they too had jewels of their own."

Young Store Per acquired a violin and developed such interests, likely with encouragement and assistance from his parents. They were not insensitive rustics, oblivious of the culture of their country. Residents of Tjernagel went to Bergen to sell fish, buy essentials and a few luxuries, visit friends, and to experience elements of their country's culture. It is probable that Store Per heard and admired Bull's virtuosity in Bergen where at least some concerts of the world-class artist were inexpensive. Did Store Per play a Hardanger fiddle, a standard four-stringed violin, or both? One clue is that Tjernagel musicians of the next generation invariably referred to his instrument as a violin. There is no record of how Store Per acquired his instrument or learned to play it.

He must have learned Hordaland tunes from older violinists of the area. One of them mentored him; it may have been his father.

Per developed a repertoire that included folk melodies, dance music, hymns, and a full range of music that came from the countryside. In fact many of the best-loved Norwegian hymn melodies were adapted from folk tunes. Gregarious and fun loving, Store Per enjoyed wedding celebrations that lasted for days, changed moods, and sometimes turned raucous. As musicians played fast-tempo "Hallings" in 2/4 or 6/8 beat, athletic young men demonstrated their strength and agility. This form of dance took its name from Hallingdal in southern Norway where gymnastics was valued highly. During intricate "Spring Dances" the fiddler's role was to lead and respond so effectively as to partner with couples on the dance floor.

Nehemias attended a wedding celebration where "untamed" young people demonstrated "such a disregard for anything resembling prudery" that their actions "partook of license." Store Per's reputation spread as a strapping, good-natured fiddler—the life of the party.

Lars and Helga's children had additional outlets for their musical talents. All members of the family loved to sing. Moster Church often echoed with vocal as well as instrumental music emanating from them. "To this hoary old stone structure Rev. Tormodsater kindly took me in his boat," wrote Nehemias after his 1892 trip to Norway, "for here I knew that father had been confirmed, and here his elder sister Helga had lifted up her glorious voice which stood out above all the others." Here also was heard Ole Andreas' accordion "and, not to be forgotten, his brother Peder's violin performances."

A tale told to this writer at Tjernagel July 5, 1983, by Ole Andreas Olson Tjernagel, a descendant of Store Per's sister Barbru, illustrates Per's budding physical prowess. It dates from a time when officials assigned residents of the Tjernagel farms to the church at Sveio, approachable by a footpath. Near the church were huge boulders which Store Per one night rearranged with his bare hands. With the largest of them he blocked the path to the church. When the pastor came down the trail the next day he was not puzzled for a moment but remarked, "Store Per must have been here!" Although mischievous, this antic could be laughed off as a boyish prank.

Across a short expanse of water from the Tjernagel North farm is Tjernagelsholmen, an island of six and a half acres with grazing land and peat deposits similar to those on the mainland. From Viking times ships waited out

storms in the cove between the island and the mainland. This offshore setting became a place for people to meet and trade. Exactly when the first watering hole appeared on the island to offer libations and shelter to traders, sailors, and travelers is lost to history.

Details commence in 1738 when a nonresident, Henning Irgens, received a permit to operate an inn on Tjernagelsholmen. Without benefit of the required government permit, a legendary widow, Anna Storksdtr, was already conducting business on the island that conflicted with Irgens' rights. She served spirituous liquors and bought and sold salted fish. For years she evaded her legal responsibilities. Subpoenaed for illegal sale of "beer, brandy, and salt," Storksdtr came to terms and paid the fees one year, then lapsed into her old habits. Through the decades, goings-on at Tjernagelsholmen wagged tongues on the mainland.

During Store Per's youth and early manhood, a tavern, a store, and a shipping company operated on the island. The Larsons were strategically located to observe changes of ownership of these businesses and the comings and goings of their clientele. Thus, early in life Store Per observed people whose lifestyles differed from those of the farmers on the mainland. He and his siblings learned how to comport themselves around strangers, including people who exercised no restraint in taking their drams.

One day in June 1844, a roving band of unruly young men known as the Valborg gang came to the Lien farm a short distance across the water from Tjernagelsholmen. A drunken member of the gang entered Kjersteen's home and attempted to rape her fourteen-year-old daughter Anna Marie. A fistfight ensued between the toughs and the girl's distraught father, Phillipus, assisted by Haldor Tjernagel. Help arrived "from Tjernagel" whereupon Phillipus and his allies "subdued the gang and tied them up." Lars and his sons were the nearest and most eligible males at Tjernagel North to lend assistance. Eighteen-year-old Store Per likely tested his mettle that day protecting his cousin Anna Marie. The gang members spent an uncomfortable night before being marched before the justice of the peace the next day.

At the approach of the summer solstice the next year, 1845, Store Per was out one night with a young woman named Johanne Johannesdatter Kinn. This is an enchanting time of year in Norway. Dormant no longer, nature stages a contest for supremacy between energy and beauty. The fjords teem with spring herring, trout climb the mountain streams, and the *saeters* explode with wildflowers. When young couples are carried along by the rhythms of nature consequences are likely.

The relationship between Peder and Johanne did not result in marriage, but it did result in the birth of a male child March 12, 1846. Faithful Kjersteen, the infant's great aunt, served as midwife. Finnas Parish records show that eleven days later the baby was christened Peder. Store Per acknowledged his paternity, but available sources do not reveal whether, in the parlance of the day, he "paid for" his son or played a role in his life. Communications with Johanne's descendants in 2007 revealed that the young mother married Mathias Jakobson Kallevik, a widower, October 24, 1847. Johanne raised Peder, along with her husband's son Ola in a blended family that also included children that the couple had together. We shall encounter Peder Pederson again near the end of this narrative.

Store Per took to the sea. Precisely when he did cannot be dated, but it would not be surprising if the timing coincided with his indiscretion. For several years he worked as a sailor aboard ships plying the sea-lanes of northern Europe. He learned that the ocean is merciless and makes no apologies. In the words of his nephew Nehemias, "it asks no one to ride its heaving back and those who do must take the natural consequences."

Norway's number one export at mid-century was west-coast spring herring. According to Harald Hamre of the Stavanger Maritime Museum, "The enormously rich herring shoals that came to the coast every year between 1808 and 1870 were the basis for a shipping traffic involving hundreds of vessels between South-West Norway and the coasts of the Baltic Sea." Exports reached their peak in the 1840s with annual production of as many as 700,000 barrels of salted herring. Sweden, Prussia, and Russia each imported about a third of Norway's supply of this nutritious product.

From his earliest days Store Per was familiar with the "catching" end of the herring industry. Vessels that brought herring to Baltic ports returned to Norway with grain, hemp, and flax. During the age of sail the latter two were essential to Norway's fleet and shipping industry — hemp for making rope and flax for making canvas. The Baltic trade entailed more than the exchange of goods. It also fostered cultural contacts. Young men from Tjernagel, Store Per among them, made friends in distant ports.

Some young men engaged in nautical pursuits that determined the pattern of their lives. Born in 1820 at Tjernagel South, Jokum Christenson Tjernagel, Store Per's cousin, is a case in point. "When sixteen years of age he became a sailor, being chiefly on the Baltic." Through his father Christen, brother of Kjersteen and Helga, Jokum inherited the entrepreneurial inclinations of his grandfather Peder Andersson Tjernagel. As he matured Jokum assumed responsibilities and took initiatives that eventually led to commanding, building, and owning ships on the Great Lakes in North America. Even when he was a young man, people at Sveio recognized Jokum's abilities and valued his counsel.

The complex of ropes, pulleys, and canvas aboard sailing vessels required knowledge, strength, and dexterity. While "learning the ropes," young sailors drew the worst jobs and were cursed and cuffed by captains and old tars, many of whom drank too much alcohol. According to the unwritten law of the sea, junior seamen must bear the onus without complaint. This rankled Store Per.

Jokum's younger half brother, Endre Christenson Tjernagel, related several incidents that occurred during the late 1840s or early 1850s when he and Store Per held sailor's credentials from the Sea Commissioner at Haugesund, seventeen miles south of Tjernagel. Younger and smaller than Store Per, Endre drew galley or kitchen duty on a voyage to Gothenburg, Sweden. Before he had gotten his sea legs he stumbled and fell in rough seas while carrying a platter of victuals. A "broadside of blows" from the captain was his reward.

On another voyage Endre and Store Per served as crew members aboard the sloop *Nesha* whose home port was on Bomlo Island. A sloop is a sailing vessel, usually with a single mast and topsail, commonly used in the coastal trade or for fishing. Sloops carried "drag-anchors" of several hundred pounds, attached to heavy iron chains. When a ship was in danger of being blown ashore and broken up in such places as *Sletten* the captain lowered sail and shouted: "All hands on deck!" Then, all together, the crew picked up the drag-anchor, threw it overboard, and prayed that it would hold the ship in deep water until the wind shifted or the storm passed.

Captains tended to be brave, decisive, and competitive men. They had to be, to survive the angry waters of the North and Baltic Seas. The captain of the *Nesha* was no exception. Moreover, he maintained a rivalry with another ship captain. One day when the two were docked near Bergen the rival spotted a man named Rejanes from Stavanger, reputed to be the reigning strongman of western Norway. After making arrangements with Rejanes, the rival challenged the *Nesha* captain to designate a member of his crew to compete in a test of strength. Store Per got the nod.

The contest involved lifting a large drag-anchor from the deck, a feat the sailors deemed impossible by one man. The captain whose man proved the weaker was to forfeit a bottle of Burgundy. Rejanes tried first and "not only lifted the huge iron but shifted its position," reported Endre. "Per, who was younger and less experienced nevertheless duplicated the feat." Given the stalemate, Endre did not know what became of the wine, but the disappointed young sailor recalled that he was "left without a taste."

That same evening Store Per accompanied his new friend Rejanes to a dance hall, the floor of which was laid on springs. Here the local swains made the mistake of insulting the two strong men with the label *Stril*, a derogatory term for fishermen from the Bergen coast. Not only was the designation incorrect (at the time they were sailors), but Rejanes was from Stavanger and Store Per from Sveio. "As the offenders persisted in their taunting, being perhaps jealous of the two handsome strangers, Rejanes asked his companion if they [had] not better throw them out." Store Per replied, "*Ja.*" Out the window they went, "head foremost in quick succession, big strapping fellows though they were, twelve in all." Whether the two had sufficient rapport with the ladies to test the springy dance floor Endre left to the imagination.

The next morning a shipmate shamed Store Per, and then fled. Store Per did not give chase, fearing the consequences of his own temper and strength were the man to fall into his clutches. Needing an outlet for his pent-up emotions, Per "belabored with his fists a nearby tree till the bark was stripped clean and his wrath appeased." Usually easygoing, Store Per once told Endre that he could remember only one other occasion when he was angered "nigh unto complete loss of self-control." We shall come to that episode late in Store Per's life.

Jokum, Store Per, Endre, and Ole Andreas traveled frequently between Norwegian and Baltic ports. When they did they passed through Gothenburg, Sweden's main port, strategically located at the opening to the Baltic. When Nehemias sailed from Norway to Germany in 1893 he stirred his emotions by recalling that over these waters "touching Norway, Denmark, Sweden, Germany and Russia" his father, Ole Andreas, came in his youth "on fishing expeditions or in transporting freight cargoes."

The Gothenburg wharves were infested with thugs and fraught with temptations. The Norwegian boys learned how to defend themselves and protect their ships. Store Per's physique was an advantage, but when Endre drew guard duty he was "kept in agony" lest thieves outwit him "and make away with the property he had been set to guard." Temptations abounded: "Pretty women with beautiful silken headdresses," recalled Endre, "would hover near with saucy lips and seductive smiles." Some begged sailors to "take their dainty 'kerchiefs in exchange for hemp rope-ends, which they unraveled and sold at a good profit to shipbuilders."

Wooden ships and wooden containers require maintenance. While their ship or the water casks in the hold were under repair at Gothenburg the gregarious boys from Tjernagel became acquainted with a cooper, Carl Magnus Johannesen, a personable Swede a few months older than Store Per. Steps in the development of lasting friendships came when Carl Magnus accompanied his Norwegian friends on visits to Tjernagel. He wintered with them at least once and enjoyed Christmas festivities and *julekake* with their families.

Long remembered were the trinkets Norwegian sailors brought back for children, and the more valuable gifts they gave to their mothers, wives, and sweethearts. Most prized were silver jewelry and tableware that came from Baltic countries.

Dramatic adventures at sea and raucous escapades on shore constituted a small fraction of a working sailor's life. Nearly all Norwegian sailors honed spitting to a fine art and walked "as if wrongly ballasted," reported Nehemias. Both phenomena resulted, at least in part, from the "poison-charged" black tobacco they chewed, "strong enough . . . to capsize a steer."

Sources are silent on whether Store Per took his violin aboard ship to counteract monotony on long voyages. He probably did, and added tunes from distant lands to his repertoire. Later, when he crossed the Atlantic as a passenger he played frequently.

As a member of Norway's merchant marine Store Per visited ports in foreign lands, made friends in far off places, and became aware of other cultures. He expanded his horizons. Scant details survive from this part of his life. However, he learned how to cope in unfamiliar surroundings and gained valuable experience while living and working with people beyond Tjernagel. It was a hard life of low pay, poor working conditions, and long absences from home. Ole Andreas made a three-year voyage before he reached the age of twenty.

Could commercial fishing become a desirable occupation for Store Per?

From boyhood he knew how to net herring near home. Nehemias accompanied his cousin Johan, Barbru's oldest son, on such a venture in a bay of Bomlo Fjord in 1910. "I gazed around at the lovely scenery as the morning sun burnished the cliffs and crags with gold," he wrote, "and I heard the distant tinkling of sheep bells, the dairymaid's call across the fjord." Using "water telescopes," Store Per's nephews saw darting herring beneath the surface. Then, "A furious, rushing sound, somewhat like escaping steam, but with more of the note of a living voice in it, burst upon our ears." Johan smiled knowingly about the unusual scene they were about to witness. A hungry whale was closing in on the herring. The prey broke toward shore, "scared to death of the fearful monster blubbering at their heels, who could swallow them by the bushel." However, they were destined for another fate. Several hundred bushels of herring scurried into Johan's waiting nets; "a wonderful sight they were when penned up."

Cod fishing required entirely different methods. For centuries, the cod industry followed a pattern established by the Hanseatic League of German merchants at Bergen.

Vessels with crews of up to five men left early in the year
for the Lofton Islands where they built crude base camps.
They caught cod with hook and line, gutted and
sometimes split the fish, dried them on wooden racks,
and brought them back to Bergen for shipment to other
European countries. After soaking in lie water, some of
the cod became Norwegian *lutefisk*. There is no evidence
that Tjernagel men participated in this sector of the cod
industry, except possibly as hired hands on the ships or
stevedores on the docks.

They did, however, find ways to bring in catches of
marketable "stockfish." In 1892 Nehemias Tjernagel
learned how they did it from relatives on Bomlo Island, a
father and son crew about to depart "with their great
sailship on a North Sea fishing cruise." On long summer
days they sailed hundreds of miles northward until they
encountered a shoal of cod, mackerel, or pollack. Then

they fished around the clock with baited drop lines. Two weeks might be required to fill the barrels in the hold with salted fish. "When full they hurry home as fast as the wind will take them, disposing of their wares and taking snatches of neglected sleep at any or all hours, night or day." Then they race back to repeat the cycle until the days shortened and the sea became hazardous. It was exhausting work but they experienced enough success to keep going. On recent expeditions the twosome claimed to have taken 400 barrels of mackerel which they "caused to be shipped and sold at a good profit in American markets."

Regardless of the species caught, independent fishermen faced a dilemma. "Often the fishing is but poor," explained Nehemias, "while at other times it is almost too good, with an opposite effect on prices which dwindle to nearly nothing, so that there is hardly more profit from plenty than from scarcity." A generation earlier Store Per too understood the law of supply and demand. He was not optimistic about making a steady living as a commercial fisherman even if he could acquire a sloop and enjoy ample catches. Moreover, the work was hazardous, "the death-toll being large, and many are the widows and orphans in Norway who look askance at the sea."

On June 22, 1850, tragedy struck the Larsons of Tjernagel North. Family records show that Store Per's older brother, Johannes, died on this day at age twenty-six, but include no information as to the place or cause of death. Finnas Parish and cemetery records make no mention of a funeral or a burial, nor is Johannes' name found in parish departure records. The most plausible explanation is that he died at sea some distance from home, likely on a North Sea fishing expedition.

Store Per knew that the sea was unforgiving. With each passing year, life as a sailor or fisherman held less and less appeal.

What were his prospects of farming in his native land? The way of life attracted him, but the family did not have enough land to subdivide. Attempting to make a living off the leased land at Lien was out of the question; his parents had already tried that. As the oldest male in the family following his brother's death, Per's rights to the Tjernagel North farm had priority over the rights of his siblings. This was the law under Norway's policy of *Odelsloven*. However, his parents needed the Tjernagel North farm to support his siblings as well as themselves. Larsine, their youngest, would not turn eighteen until 1860. More of an aggravation than a practical consideration was the cloud upon the land title dating back to feudal times and Catholic Norway. Prospects of settling down soon and comfortably on ancestral land with an unencumbered title seemed remote.

Let us imagine that Store Per took stock of his life on his twenty-sixth birthday, February 12, 1852, by comparing his circumstances with those of two of his closest friends, *Taalige* Lars Henderson and Carl Magnus Johannesson, the Swedish cooper. After living three years in America, *Taallige* Lars had returned to Norway in 1850 to take a wife. He soon spoke of settling his family on a farm in Illinois. Carl too had America on his mind. Coming from an Old World artisan tradition, "opportunity" loomed larger in his mind than did a goal of acquiring land.

During visits to Tjernagel, Carl kept company with Gunilde Haldorsdatter, one of Per's many cousins. A son was born to them out of wedlock in 1851. Committed to each other, they too regarded America as the place to establish their family. Store Per's mind could not resist linking marriage, America, and land acquisition.

The conventional wisdom in Sveio was that if a man wanted to marry he should set sail for Bomlo. Store Per found female companionship closer to home. When not at sea he kept company with a strong and healthy young woman he had known since childhood, a half sister of Endre, his sailing companion. Her name was Malene and she lived on the Tjernagel South farm, a half-mile from his home. Affection grew between the cousins. Their plans converged and they concluded that they needed each other to carry them out.

The decision of whether to make a living on land or at sea now came easily for Store Per. If he had not already rejected the occupations of sailor and fisherman for other reasons, Store Per now rejected them as incompatible with marriage. He wanted to become a landowning farmer but knew that prospects of acquiring sufficient land at Tjernagel to support a wife and family in a manner he deemed adequate were dim.

As of early 1852, Store Per and his betrothed shared with other Sveio residents the dream of departing for America and acquiring a farm. America, "that country of wealth, that dream of delight, that place whither they so eagerly desired to go, and whither their brothers and cousins and friends had gone before."

Store Per and Malene harbored no animosity toward church or government in Norway but could not avoid the conclusion that the Old Country with its stratified society, vestiges of feudalism, and small rocky fields had grown weary of her inhabitants. Why not marry, go to America, acquire land, and live out their lives where people did not feel the heavy hand of the past—a nation with no subjects, only citizens.

Not until the discovery of oil in the North Sea in the 1960s did Norway begin to become the wealthy nation it is today. In the twenty-first century it consistently ranks in the top bracket of nations with respect to standard of living.

Chapter Four

MARRIAGE AND VOYAGE
TO AMERICA

The pioneers of every nation yet to be —
The first low wash of waves where soon
shall roll a human sea.

The harbor at Tjernagel provided a window to the outside world for the people of that place. Precisely when the first person landed on the dock with news of inexpensive, fertile land in the American west cannot now be determined. The big picture, however, is clear.

The year prior to Store Per's birth marked the beginning of group migration from Norway to America. It began July 4, 1825, at Stavanger, down the coast from Tjernagel, with the departure of the sloop *Restoration* with forty-five passengers and a crew of seven, bound for New York. Most of the Sloopers, as they became known, were Quakers, Quaker sympathizers, or followers of the lay preacher Hans Nielsen Hauge (1771-1824) who felt oppressed by the state church of Norway.

The *Restoration* docked at New York City October 9. According to the city's *Daily Advertiser*: "The appearance of such a party of strangers, coming from so distant a country and in a vessel of a size apparently ill calculated for a voyage across the Atlantic, could not but excite an unusual degree of interest." In particular, the Norwegians' clothing caught the journalist's eye. "Those

53

who came from the farms are dressed in coarse cloths of domestic manufacture, of a fashion different from the American." In contrast, those who hailed from Stavanger wore "calicos, ginghams and gay shawls, imported, we presume, from England."

The Sloopers soon departed via the Hudson River and the nearly completed Erie Canal for Kendall, New York, on the shore of Lake Ontario. Here they acquired land and established a colony according to a plan brokered by their advance man, Cleng Peerson. A few members of the original party lived out their lives at Kendall; most did not.

Restless of mind and body, Peerson walked westward. One day in 1833 while exploring LaSalle County, Illinois, he fell asleep under a tree. Like Jacob of the Old Testament, he dreamed. In his dream Peerson saw "the wild prairie changed into a cultivated region, teeming with all kinds of grain and fruit most beautiful to behold; . . . splendid houses and barns stood all over the land, occupied by a rich, prosperous and happy people. Alongside the fields of waving grain large herds of cattle were feeding." Cleng regarded the vision as a sign from God that Norwegians should come and settle in the Fox River Valley. Most of the Sloopers did so and acquired land at bargain prices in what became known as the Fox River Settlement.

Still restless, Peerson moved on to Missouri and then to Texas. Nevertheless, his dream of Norwegian prosperity on the Illinois prairie assumed a life of its own. What transformed the dream into reality were hundreds of "*Amerika letters*" that circulated first in the coastal villages and valleys of western Norway and then deeper in the interior. They passed from house to house and parish to parish "and many were in this way induced to think of America and emigration."

Ole Bull, the violinist, did his share to publicize America too. In the midst of a busy career as performer and composer he founded a colony, Oleana, in north central Pennsylvania in 1852 to which he hoped to attract thousands of Norwegians. Such plans did not materialize. The Oleana bubble soon burst and "the explosion was accompanied by a roar of laughter in Norway and in America." Despite Bull's best intentions, the lasting legacy of the ill-managed colony was the song *Oleana* by a clever satirist, Ditman Meidell. Here, translated into English, are its opening verses.

> I'm off to Oleana. I'm turning from my doorway,
> No chains for me, I'll say good-bye to slavery in Norway.
> Ole — Ole — Ole — oh! Oleana!
> Ole — Ole — Ole — oh! Oleana!
>
> They give you land for nothing in jolly Oleana,
> And grain comes leaping from the ground
> in floods of golden manna.
>
> The grain it does the threshing, it pours into the sack, Sir,
> You make a quart of whiskey from each one
> without expense, Sir.
> . . . .
> And little roasted piggies, with manners quite demure, Sir,
> They ask you, Will you have some ham?
> And then you say, Why, sure, Sir!

Store Per and Malene learned about America from many sources but they did not fall victim to Bull's Oleana propaganda. Current information came from close relatives. Malene's oldest brother, Peder Christenson Tjernagel, became the first member of the family to come to the United States. He, his wife Berthe Marie, and their two young sons arrived in New York aboard the *Favoriten* June 28, 1849, and promptly struck out for the Fox River Settlement. Heart breaking news soon reached relatives back in Sveio. Asiatic cholera struck the young mother and she died July 20.

Despite the setback, Peder persevered and soon acquired the first of his several farms. A good natured and generous man, his home became "the landing place of all relatives when they came and they were always welcome and there was always room." Malene and her brother enlisted the services of others to communicate across the Atlantic because they could neither read nor write.

A batch of *"Amerika letters"* from *Tante* Kjersteen and her family determined Store Per and Malene's initial destination in America. Early in 1850 Phillipus and Kjersteen sold the Lien farm that they had owned for thirty years. They arrived at New York City aboard the *Therese* August 28. Documents they carried on the journey are in the possession of their descendants in Des Moines, Iowa. With the mature couple were their sons, Knut and Peder, and their daughter Helga. On the same vessel, but listed in another party, was their married daughter, Anna Marie, her husband Michael Lie, and their infant daughter. The party proceded to Koshkonong in eastern Dane County, Wisconsin, a Norwegian settlement dating from 1840. The Lie family did not remain long because Koshkonong land was expensive and they wanted to get on with their lives.

By the time Store Per and Malene were finalizing their travel plans, Michael Lie had moved his family to a new farm in *Indi-landet* (Indian land) near Waupaca, Wisconsin. Here in the pinewoods land could be had for the minimum government price of $1.25 an acre. In fact, some settlers were squatting, clearing land, and selling timber without paying any money at all.

Letters Anna Marie mailed back to Sveio must have waxed eloquent about the newest Norwegian settlement and how to get there. One could travel every inch of the way from Tjernagel to *Indi-landet*—by water! Following the Atlantic crossing, steamboats carried immigrants from New York City up the Hudson River to the head of the Erie Canal. Then canal boats transported them across the State of New York, through a series of locks, and deposited them on Lake Erie. From there it would be smooth sailing through the Great Lakes to Green Bay and, presumably, also upstream to Waupaca.

A Norwegian sailship company reportedly booked passengers for the entire trip and promised to "set them off at Waupaca" where cheap land was available. Energetic young people anxious to own property could hardly resist such prospects. Events moved Malene and Store Per along at a rapid pace.

Three major changes marked their lives in 1852—marriage on April 13, departure from Norway a week later, and transition to life in America. The first two are chronicled in the remainder of this chapter, the third in the next.

Malene's girlhood home at Tjernagel South bustled with wedding preparations that spring. Her layered trousseau would incorporate the best fabrics her family could afford, trimmed with colorful Hordaland designs. Over this on her wedding day Malene would don either a white gown or a festive apron decorated with a band of cutwork embroidery. Norwegian bridal crowns, steeped

in tradition and decorated with spangles and ribbons, were passed down from generation to generation. Malene's mother had died years earlier but wearing her bridal crown would link the past to the present. No trousseau was complete without a *solje*, a glittering brooch or necklace. Perhaps Store Per had one made for his bride from silver brought back from the Baltic.

Typical attire for a Hordaland groom was a hand-made wool suit with short pants and stockings that came up to the calf, a white shirt and vest, and a colorful coat ornamented with metal buttons and brocade.

We can imagine a wedding procession gathering at Malene's home on the Tjernagel South farm Tuesday, April 13, with the bride and groom in their finery taking their seats in the best horse-drawn wagon or *kariole* available. Unless Store Per did the honors himself, a fiddler friend led the procession through the countryside toward the parish church at Sveio. Along the way people joined the happy procession. Despite his lowly birth, the groom looked like a prince that day. By all accounts he was a large, handsome, and well-proportioned young man.

The day did not belong exclusively to Malene and Store Per. The bell that rang out as they approached the church also beckoned "Carl Magnus Johanessen fra Gotheborg" and "Gunilde Haldersdr Tjernagel." That is how the Rev. Johan Frederik Holst entered their names April 13, 1852, in the record of marriages at which he officiated. The two couples must have arranged a double wedding ceremony. Gunilde and Carl already had a son, Elias, seven months old—not an uncommon circumstance at the time.

In addition to exchanges of vows, a typical wedding ceremony of the time included Scripture readings, congregational singing, and pastoral advice. Pastor Holst's message likely included reference to the couples' impending departure for America and admonitions to stay faithful to Biblical truths. The State Church of Norway then opposed emigration and largely ignored the spiritual needs of Norwegians after left the country.

Following vows, the pastor's "man and wife" pronouncements, and the benediction, came hand shaking and expressions of good wishes. Store Per's mother was not present for the occasion; Helga had died the previous year. The parish register duly records the marriage of "Peder Larson Tjernagel" to "Malene Christendr Tjernagel" April 13, 1852, witnessed by Lars Jorgenson of Nordskog, a farm near Tjernagel, and Bernt Jacobsen of Sveio.

There is every reason to believe that, following the ceremony, the brides' families hosted a traditional, three-day festival to launch the couples on the voyage of life. The return to Tjernagel South would be more spirited than the outbound procession, again with a fiddler in the lead. Good beer would soon be in the offing. A field near the water's edge at Tjernagel South was known for its excellent hops.

Guests arrived in the traditional dress of their locality. The hosts supplied beer, the main course for several meals, and cake. To lighten the burden, guests brought white bread (as opposed to the dark rye bread of everyday existence), their best flat bread, *lefse*, *kringla*, and other provender.

The governor of the feast (*kjogemester*) welcomed the guests, summoned them at appropriate times to partake of food and drink, and oversaw the music, dancing, and general tone of the event. Meals lasted for hours, as there must be conviviality and second and third tables in the small quarters of Malene's home. Pleasures must not be rushed.

The breathy bellows of Ole Andreas' accordion brought fiddlers and couples to their feet for Spring Dances. Malene and Gunhilde danced with their husbands until the jingling of their spangles synchronized with the rhythm of the music and the stomping of feet. According to tradition, such frenzy warded off evil spirits so they could not inhabit the bride or diminish her happiness.

Nehemias attended a wedding festival some years later and related that the hosts poured large, gaily decorated Russian bowls of "mild and innocent" homemade beer. "The guests drank from the same bowl to the very dregs, and then it was quickly refilled, to make another round... as it was passed from hand to hand and mouth to mouth." The menu included soups, meats, and "a boatful of fresh, cooked codfish." Then came coffee and desserts such as "*lefse, kringler*, and *sukker kager*." Thus it went "from early morn till late at night; we were munching something all the time, and kept it up for three days," recalled Nehemias. Guests got little sleep, "for the old must needs talk and gossip and smoke, while the young must watch their opportunity to get acquainted, fall in love, and perform such other preliminaries as are necessary to insure future weddings."

Jovial man that he was, Store Per enjoyed the wedding feast to the full. Certainly he joined his brother and other musicians to express his happiness with his violin. There were also tender moments and undercurrents of sadness because the newlyweds and some of the guests would soon depart for America via the port of Stavanger. Store Per did not know if he would ever see his sisters again. Ole Andreas, however, already contemplated following his brother to America.

Guidebooks recommended leaving Norway in early spring so that farm people would not lose an entire growing season. Accordingly, this was the plan of a party of nine from Tjernagel. The group consisted of: Store Per and Malene; Carl Magnus Johannesen, Gunilde, and little Elias; Malene's brother Jokum Christensen Tjernagel, his wife Anna, and their son Christopher; and Malene's half brother Endre Christensen Tjernagel, a bachelor. On the same day as the wedding Pastor Holst recorded the impending emigration of these nine, with slight variations in the spelling of their names. Nehemias' 1922 account reported that, in addition to the people just mentioned, "about fifty others" from Sveio laid similar plans, including nine members each of the Nygaard and Lie families. Among the latter were Michael Lie's father, his stepmother, his siblings, and half-siblings, all of whom can be identified in the passenger list of the vessel that soon carried them across the Atlantic.

Following the wedding, Store Per and Malene spent only eight more days in their native land, not all of which could be devoted to celebrating, packing, food preparation, business details, and goodbyes. They also needed time to travel southward from Tjernagel to Stavanger. For the sailors, this would be routine; for their wives and children, perhaps not.

Accounts refer to the gargantuan wooden chest Store Per built for the voyage, complete with iron bands, lock and key, handles, and a paint job incorporating his name and destination, Waupaca, Wisconsin. Making the chest was easier than deciding what to pack into it. Necessities included his Bible, violin, bedclothes, strong clothing, tools (including those for making wooden shoes), an iron plate for baking flat bread, pots, pans, kitchen utensils, and components for a spinning wheel. Possessions that would not fit in he sold or gave away.

Many packing and food details fell to Malene who engaged in a flurry of last minute baking. Guidebooks recommended sufficient food to last twelve weeks without spoiling aboard a damp wooden ship. Ole Rynning's list included: hard rye bread which kept well, butter, cheese, milk, dried or salted meat and fish, flour, peas, cereals, potatoes, beer, coffee, tea, and sugar. For reasons of health he advised: "a little brandy, vinegar, and a couple of bottles of wine, as well as raisins and prunes to make soup for the seasick." Also some basic medicines, "salt-water soap for washing, and good fine combs." The latter were for combing out lice, common pests on ships carrying emigrants.

On the appointed day Store Per and his immediate party loaded trunks and food boxes on carts for their last trip from home to the Tjernagel wharf. His father and siblings saw him off. Casting off prompted tearful goodbyes to home and family. What entered Store Per's mind as he and his bride sailed beyond the protective cove and viewed its defining features for the last time is lost to history. As long as he could remember, Mount Siggen and those mooring spikes circled with tar had guided him home in vessels of every description from rowboats to sloops. Strand by strand, ties to the Old Country loosened, but the Tjernagel name and countless memories would be with him for life.

To deal with a treacherous expanse of water as they sailed southward, the party may have put in above Haugesund to board a larger vessel for the remainder of the voyage down coast to Stavanger. Familiar to Store Per from his years as a sailor, this bustling international port and center of the herring industry was about to take on another function. Here the *Rogaland*, a schooner of Norwegian registry, lay at anchor in preparation for carrying iron and emigrants to New York.

The ship took its name from the county immediately south of Hordaland where Stavanger is located. "The ocean schooner, queen of the seas in its day, with its sturdy lines and white flash of its canvas, has inspired many a great poet to sing its beauty." Schooners were two-masted ocean-going vessels, considerably larger than sloops, designed to carry a mainsail, a foresail, and at least one jib. Faster sailing and steam-powered vessels plied the Atlantic in the middle years of the nineteenth century, but for emigrants, schooners had the advantage of economy.

Record of the fare from Stavanger to New York City aboard the *Rogaland* has not been found. For steerage passengers, it was probably between ten and fifteen Norwegian specie dollars per adult. To put these sums in perspective, Torkel Henryson who sailed from Bergen to New York City aboard the *Kong Sverre* in 1847 reported that, prior to departure, he taught school for ten specie dollars a year plus room and board. Store Per's sister Larsine and her husband Nils Peterson each paid $26 to cross the Atlantic on the *Admiral Trumph* in 1864, but the source does not specify whether they paid in American greenbacks or more valuable Norwegian specie dollars.

The *Rogaland* had its poet. Upon the launching of the vessel in 1849 a sail-maker, O. C. Mathiesen, printed *Skonnerten Rogaland*, a poem in five verses, in the May 5 issue of a Stavanger newspaper. Here, translated into English, are the first two verses.

> Sail thou out upon the sea, out from
> thy mother's bosom, thou beautiful,
> serpent-like "Rogaland." Cut thy way
> through the billows, beat back their
> blows; and may the winds carry thee
> prosperously from coast to coast.
>
> Behold these mighty mountains and
> these cliffs, impregnable to wind and
> wave, born of the gods. Bid them
> farewell, and remember courage and
> strength have sworn allegiance to their flag.

In its three years of service the *Rogaland* had compiled an impressive record that passed the scrutiny of the sailors from Tjernagel. Together with their families, the soon-to-be emigrants watched as ropes and hooks dangled from the deck of the *Rogaland* toward small boats ladened with their trunks. Workers fastened the ropes to the trunk handles and swung the precious cargo aboard the larger vessel. Following goodbyes to friends and relatives still with them, the ninety-two passengers ferried to what would be their home for the next seven weeks. "It was a wondrous sight to see," reads an emigrant ballad: "the decks swarmed like an ant heap, kerchiefs and caps of every color—and all were bent on leaving the country." The last contact with Norwegian officialdom came in the form of a sermon preached on deck by a state minister who urged the emigrants "to live the good life and not to forget their fathers' god."

The *Rogaland* sailed for New York April 21, 1852. One emigrant wrote: "After we had lifted the anchor, our captain gave us a talk, explaining our duties, urging us to be cleanly, obedient, alert, and helpful to one another, and advising us to observe the rules posted in several places on the boat." Rules stressed the importance of sweeping, cleaning, and scrubbing to prevent the spread of disease.

The party from Tjernagel had chosen well with respect to ship and captain. They had heard of filthy, disease-generating conditions aboard emigrant ships and physical abuse of passengers by captains and crews. By law, captains were obligated to supply fresh water and stove wood for their passengers. Because of abuses, some contracts read that the captain must drink out of the same water barrels as his passengers. Seasickness could not be avoided. However, no evidence of malfeasance on the part of Captain T. C. Jonasen or the *Rogaland* crew has come down to Tjernagel posterity.

The lowest level of the ship held ballast and heavy cargo such as iron for American railroads. Heavy emigrant chests and large casks of fresh water occupied the next level. A common way of outfitting an emigrant ship was to construct sleeping berths on a third level with ranges four bunks wide, port and starboard, running from bow to stern. Some schooners were outfitted with two tiers of sleeping berths. "We'll pack you bumpkins like herring in a barrel," so went a satirical emigrant song, "'tis only an interlude twixt barrel and palace." Neither privacy partitions for families nor separate areas for men and women interrupted the cramped space. Emigrants placed items needed during the voyage in small trunks and lashed them to their beds so they would not slide away. Natural light came through skylights and hatchways, which had to be closed in rough seas. At such times and at night, lamps cast eerie shadows below deck. Steerage passengers furnished their own bedding and food.

Of the ninety-two *Rogaland* passengers only two paid for cabin passage and ate at the captain's table. Therefore at mealtime ninety people, divided into groups of various sizes, vied to use a "free-for-all" cook stove located in a shed on deck. Early in the voyage there was much to do: "supplies of smoked and salted meat and flat bread to be attended to and the first meals to be prepared; bedding to be placed on the straw heaped into the bunks; children to be cared for; and chores of various kinds to be performed." Responsible captains established routines to maintain cleanliness.

All too soon the coast disappeared and the emigrants said farewell to their native land. Upon departure, Store Per knew at least half of the passengers. Outgoing man that he was, he likely knew them all before the voyage was over. Two thirds of the passengers were male and a third female. Only fourteen of the ninety-two had reached their thirtieth birthdays; thirty-two were below the age of twenty-one. These counts are consistent with the generalization that the century-long migration of 850,000 Norwegians to America (beginning with the Sloopers in 1825, reaching its zenith in 1882, and reduced to a trickle by the national origins quota system in the mid 1920s) was largely a movement of youth.

Some of the farm people aboard the *Rogaland* had little experience on the high seas. "A typical daytime scene," reported a diarist "was that of younger women knitting and sewing, old women reading or singing songs, men staring out at the sea." However, when the ship pitched and rolled the landlubbers went below deck to retch and vomit. "One can imagine the sufferings of the wretched creatures . . . shut up in the dark room night and day," recounted a ship captain, "for the hatches were battened as the waves went over the deck continually." In the words of the *Rogaland* poet, "In the crash of the waves and the blast of the storm dwells still the God of Peace and Love." On pleasant days the crew opened the hatches to air out the hold and passengers hung their laundry on the ship's rigging.

An experienced seaman, Store Per was immune to seasickness. To his fellow passengers he likely repeated the sailor's bromide: "Focus your eyes on the horizon." From Viking times Norwegians who went to sea mixed *malurt brennevin* with mead to prevent seasickness and to cure digestive disorders. Some *Rogaland* passengers and members of the crew likely had supplies of it in their baggage. Commonly known as wormwood, it is a consciousness-altering substance that countries of the western world banned early in the twentieth century.

Based on interviews with *Rogaland* passengers years after the voyage, three of Per's nephews, brothers Lars Johan, Peder Gustav, and Nehemias Tjernagel, wrote accounts of the Atlantic crossing and continuation of the journey into the American heartland. All three featured the role played by their uncle of "enormous strength" in raising the spirits of his fellow passengers. In his 1931 account Peder Gustav introduced his hero by stating that wherever Store Per happened to be he was the life of the party. "He was an athlete of the highest order, a humorist, a musician, and to crown it all, a man with an even temperament."

"Peer had his violin with him," Peder Gustav continued, "and his masterful performances served many a time during the long tedious journey to drive away blues, and melancholia. His Spring Dances, Hallings, and other national dances . . . would lure sulking maidens out of their retreats, grouchy young men brooding over their last attack of sea sickness out of their hiding places, tired men and women from their duties, as well as squirming children." Out on the deck they stomped, some in wooden shoes and homespun dress, "to do justice to the national dances, which were so liberally and enticingly reaching out towards them from Peer's violin."

On other occasions Store Per enticed his fellow passengers to sing folk songs. "This hit the soft spot of any Norwegian," reported Peder Gustav, "because who can you find in Norway that doesn't sing? It touched the heart strings and moistened the eyes of the most stoical ones, for it reminded them so forcibly of the beautiful fjords and picturesque landscape left behind never to be seen again by most of them."

Sundays aboard the *Rogaland* were devoted to worship "and offering up thanks to the good Lord for having preserved them up to this time, and praying for His merciful guidance during the rest of their journey," wrote Peder Gustav. Then "good substantial old Lutheran hymns" resounded "with more than equal fervor to the folk songs of the previous day."

May 17, Norway's national holiday, was a day of celebration for Norwegians crossing the Atlantic. For eighty-four emigrants aboard the *Aegir* in 1837 a salvo of cannons saluted the dawn of a beautiful *Syttende Mai* in mid-Atlantic. The passengers donned their best clothes and enjoyed "a jolly skit, not untouched by sadness, of the land they had just left." At noon "the whole company . . . assembled at a festive banquet, at which, to the accompaniment of cannon, toasts were drunk to the day, to the fatherland and Liberty, and to our beloved king and his son."

Ole Rynning, author of the guidebook previously quoted, was aboard the *Aegir*. He composed a song that the passengers sang that afternoon. Here in translation is the last of its five stanzas, toasting the westward-bound emigrant:

> But though Destiny should bid him
> pitch his tent where once Bjorn and
> Leif pitched theirs, he will cherish
> always the mountains of Norway, and
> yearn with pious longing to see his
> home once more.

"In the evening," the newspaper account continued, "there was dancing; and so, amid innocent entertainment and merriment, this day . . . came to an end with the last rays of the sun, as it sank into the ocean."

A captain who corroborated accounts of merriment on the Atlantic added the sobering note that on one crossing he buried thirteen passengers at sea. Ole Rynning survived the crossing, but celebrated only one more *Syttende Mai*. He died of malaria in the fall of 1838 and is buried in a nameless grave on the Illinois prairie. For many Norwegian families, the cost of coming to America was much greater than what they paid for fares to cross the Atlantic.

At the Newfoundland banks some captains lowered sail and allowed their passengers to fish for cod. They "cast out big baited hooks attached to strong lines," one man reported, "and before many minutes one after another of the big finny tribe was landed on deck." After weeks of eating hard bread and salted fish, fresh cod was most welcome.

Following fifty-one days at sea, some good, some humdrum, others barely tolerable, a pilot came aboard and docked the *Rogaland* at New York City June 10—one of fifty-nine dockings of Norwegian vessels at American ports in 1852. Captain Jonasen reported to port authorities that he had not lost a single person at sea. Truly happy, his passengers were also very tired.

Chapter Five

TRANSITION TO LIFE
IN AMERICA

From every degree of latitude and of longitude, and from every isle and continent, under the whole heaven, the flood of emigration has powered in upon the United States. . . . There has been nothing like it since the encampments of the Roman empire, or the tents of the crusaders.

Neither the Statue of Liberty nor the federal immigration station at Ellis Island yet existed when Store Per arrived in the New World. He began his transition to life in America at Castle Garden, a facility of the State of New York at the tip of Manhattan Island near the mouth of the Hudson River. The official who compiled the list of ninety-two passengers as they disembarked from the *Rogaland* recorded numbers seventy-two and seventy-three as: "Peder Larsen Lien," age twenty-six, and "Malena Lien," age twenty-five. The enumerator must have assumed that both had been born at Lien.

Becoming an American involved more than walking down the gangplank onto Manhattan Island and into the streets of New York City. There was much to see and learn. Here Norwegian farm people saw Blacks for the first time among the dock workers, draymen, and multitudes who bustled about the city. From his first day in the New World struggles raged within Store Per. Old habits and ways must yield to new ways of speaking and functioning.

The struggle with language surfaced immediately and intensified during the trip into the interior. "A correct use of the English language is the first and chief stamp of American nationality," wrote an early historian of the Norwegian-American experience, "the key without which the foreigner cannot enter the spirit of American life and institutions." Store Per understood this and had every intention of participating in the life of his adopted country. This would not happen overnight.

According to the parallel accounts of Peder Gustav and Nehemias, Store Per and all but one of his immediate party knew but four English words: "yes, no," and "Waupaca, Wisconsin." The exception, Malene's brother whom the enumerator recorded as "Jocum Chr. Tjernagel," could speak a little English. He had been at sea since age sixteen and was not naïve. Relatives and peers respected Jokum and relied upon him for negotiating travel arrangements. But language mastery involves more than the ability to understand directions and buy food. It also involves the ability to express subtle feelings and emotions. Ordinarily, it takes years for an adult to acquire that level of proficiency in a new language. Store Per was no exception. Sometimes when his halting English proved inadequate, he expressed his emotions with his violin or with his physical strength. A line in an emigrant ballad reads: "And most of all I miss my native tongue, with its sharp, clear tones like the clash of swords."

We know the route and modes of transportation the Tjernagel party used from Castle Garden into the interior, but precious little about timing and what transpired along the way. A few details center on Malene's half brother, number ninety-two in the *Rogaland* passenger list, "Endre Christiensen Tjernagel," age eighteen, who ran out of money in New York. Endre sold his trunk and contents and considered hiring out as a sailor on a ship bound for South America. But Store Per and Malene intervened, "gave him fare money and induced him to come west."

Fast-talking hucksters preyed upon hapless immigrants on the wharves and in the streets of New York City. Some ship captains helped their passengers bypass these rogues by arranging transportation into the interior. In 1849, Captain Westergaard of the *Favoriten* not only made arrangements for a steamboat to carry Malene's brother Peder and his party up the Hudson River at a good price, but he also accompanied them as far as Troy, New York, a distance of 180 miles. Captain Jonasen of the *Rogaland* may have assisted the Tjernagel party in this way too, or perhaps Jokum made the arrangements. Nehemias' account implies that the trip to Waupaca went smoothly—up to a point. "A little steamer" carried them from Castle Garden 144 miles up the Hudson to Albany where they could no longer discern the Atlantic tide.

On this leg of the journey they steamed past Weehawken, where Alexander Hamilton fell in a duel with Aaron Burr; through the Palisades, where the Hudson River school of artists honed their skills; and across Tappen Bay, associated with Benedict Arnold's act of treason. Farther north they cruised past Sing Sing, where the State of New York housed its dangerous criminals; by West Point, home of the United States Military Academy; and past many Revolutionary War sites. The day afforded opportunities for learning about American history and culture, if only the Tjernagel nine had the language skills to comprehend.

From Albany they headed west "by canal boat to Buffalo," reported Nehemias. A sufficient number of *Rogaland* passengers likely pooled resources to engage their own boat for the trip across the State of New York on the Erie Canal. As was true at each transfer point along the way, the able bodied men, several of them experienced stevedores, reloaded the trunks and baggage into vessels suitable for the next leg of the journey. American canal boats were of a design unfamiliar to the Norwegians, even to the sailors in the group. Typically, they measured eighty feet long, fifteen feet wide, and were outfitted to be towed by horses or mules. Passenger boats (as opposed to freighters) had covers to shield people from the elements.

The challenge of the canal builders had been to negotiate an ascent of 568 feet from the Hudson River to Buffalo on Lake Erie. As first constructed the canal was 363 miles long, four feet deep, and forty-two feet wide at the top. "Owing to the fact that the canal ascended and descended to avoid expensive cuttings or embankments, the total lockage was increased to about 700 feet."

During construction scoffers had called the $7,000,000 project "Clinton's Ditch" after New York Governor De Witt Clinton who consistently backed it. Now, twenty-seven years after completion, there were no scoffers. User fees had paid for construction several times over and had financed improvements to the system. The canal stimulated the economies of towns along the route (Albany, Troy, Little Falls, Utica, Rome, Syracuse, Rochester, Lockport and Buffalo) and catapulted New York City above all rival cities on the Atlantic coast.

More important for Store Per who planned to farm, the canal tapped a vast agricultural hinterland that was shipping hundreds of canal boats eastward, each ladened with 3,500 bushels of wheat.

Journalist Horace Greeley once reported that people traveled the Erie Canal a mile and a half an hour for a cent and a half a mile. By mid century the boats moved faster, but the top speed remained the walking gait of a horse. Therefore, passengers of at least modest means abandoned the canal in favor of roads and railroads. In contrast to travel by rail, canal travel remained democratic and inexpensive. As of 1852 most immigrants traveling with their families and possessions still used the canal. A Utica newspaper reported a company of thirty or forty "comfortably stowed away in one of the large covered canal boats, as chirp as a flock of blackbirds." The group might have been the Tjernagels.

The valley of the Mohawk offered lush scenery, but the eighteen aqueducts and eighty-three locks of the Erie Canal captivated people unaccustomed to such dramatic alterations of nature. The stone aqueduct over the Genesee River at Rochester and two sets of five "combined locks" at Lockport (one set for each direction) constituted engineering marvels of the age.

As the Tjernagel party inched its way westward they heard a cacophony of languages emanating from other boats, met scores of eastbound grain boats, and heard swine squealing their way to market. Such sounds mingled with staccato bugle blasts from impatient boat captains and welcomed newcomers to bustling America. When shadows lengthened, the tinkle of bells from boarding houses and hotels summoned weary travelers. However, the Norwegians ate their own food and slept for free under the stars or in their rented boat.

Upon arrival at Buffalo there were options. It is certain that the 1852 party "laid over" at some point or points because they arrived at Castle Garden June 10 and did not reach the vicinity of Waupaca until August 12. Under normal circumstances two weeks would suffice for the trip. But Asiatic cholera stalked the emigrant routes that summer. Some parties halted until threats diminished or were quarantined by municipalities; others deliberately paused to earn money.

Thus far in their journey from Stavanger the Tjernagels duplicated the route of the Sloopers twenty-seven years earlier. Perhaps the two newlywed couples persuaded their party to warehouse the heavy baggage at Buffalo and take an excursion to Niagara Falls only twenty miles distant. (When he came to America in 1856 Store Per's brother Ole Andreas visited the falls.) If good weather and good fortune prevailed, it would have been difficult for young men and women to resist this widely acclaimed natural wonder. They might also have proceeded on to Kendall, New York, to visit fellow Norwegians who still lived in or near the colony founded by the Sloopers in 1825.

A less likely possibility is that, from some point along the canal or at its terminus, they dropped down to Oleana near Coudersport in Potter County, Pennsylvania. Ole Bull of Bergen was in the United States in 1852 and his real estate scheme was generating its maximum publicity. No less a Norwegian-American than even-keeled Rev. Jacob Aal Ottesen got caught up in the Oleana excitement.

Historian Theodore C. Blegen relates that a rogue who impersonated this venerable pastor ingratiated himself with a party of Norwegian immigrants traveling the Erie Canal to Buffalo. He prayed with them in their own language, helped them, "and finally offered to change their gold, which he said had lost value because of the great production of California gold." Then he disappeared with more than $300 of their precious money. It was a well-timed and executed hoax; the real Pastor Otteson did travel the Erie Canal on his way west in September 1852.

Available sources are silent on whether Store Per and his party avoided sickness, fraud, and accidents on their journey into the interior. Likewise, they are silent on where the party spent a month and half that cannot be accounted for between New York City and Waupaca. Nehemias simply recorded that from Buffalo they traveled "to Green Bay, Wisconsin on a steamer."

"The Quay," a building on the shore of Lake Erie at Buffalo is where passengers bought tickets and boarded ships for the voyage to Detroit. It "surpassed any thing I ever yet saw for hubbub and noise," reported Massachusetts aristocrat and historian Francis Parkman. As early as 1845 three vessels a day were departing for Detroit during the summer travel season. Parkman's $7 ticket gave him access to comforts beyond those available to deck passengers who paid the minimum fare.

A recent Harvard graduate, Parkman came west to gather material for his book, *The Conspiracy of Pontiac*. His journal documents how an impetuous Boston Brahmin viewed "a host of Norwegian emigrants" on their way

TRANSITION TO LIFE IN AMERICA

west. They were "very diminutive—very ugly—very stupid and brutal in appearance—and very dirty. They appear to me less intelligent and as ignorant as the Indians." Besides Norwegians and Indians, the Harvard historian steamed through Lake Erie on the same vessel with a "motley swarm of passengers of all nations." America was in the making before his very eyes, but the historian's mind was fixed on the previous century.

Regardless of how upper class Americans viewed them, immigrants who plied the Great Lakes for five summer days or a week generally enjoyed the experience. One key member of the Tjernagel party, Jokum, was so impressed that he made his living for the remainder of his life on the largest body of fresh water in the world. Knud Knudsen, a Norwegian who was not part of the Tjernagel party, observed that cooks and stewards on Great Lakes vessels "are all negroes." He found them to be "exceedingly good natured and polite . . . so that I think they surpass all other nations in good nature."

Marine technology advanced rapidly at mid-century. The side-paddler *Atlantic*, 267 feet in length, steamed from Buffalo to Detroit in just sixteen-and-a-half hours in 1849. Its huge engines required enormous quantities of fuel. As of 1852 all Great Lakes steamers burned cordwood, yet most still carried masts fitted with sails and jibs. Steamers were becoming larger and faster with the trend away from paddle-wheelers to schooners with efficient screw propellers designed by the Swede, John Ericsson. His countryman, Carl Magnus, certainly pointed this out to Store Per, his Norwegian friend and companion. According to specialists at the Minnesota Historical Society, the wooden Palace Steamers of the period "were the most beautifully-appointed craft ever built on the Lakes."

If the Tjernagels navigated Lake Erie on the *Atlantic,* they were among its last passengers. On August 20, 1852, this speedy side-paddler collided with propeller-driven *Ogdensburgh* "off Land Point, Lake Erie" and sank with the loss of 131 passengers.

Narrow channels linking the Great Lakes limited the size and draft of steamboats. This was particularly true of the straits and shallows between Lake Erie and Lake Huron. Here the course was up the Detroit River to the city of that name, a bustling metropolis in 1852 that extended for two miles along the west bank of the river. Low lying French buildings were giving way to substantial American homes, churches, and public buildings. The pattern of land ownership of the prior French regime made sense to people from Tjernagel. Long, narrow lots fronting on the river provided access to markets for the farmers, tradesmen, and industrialists who owned them.

When they put in to take on fuel or transfer to other vessels the Tjernagels came into contact with Indians and mixed bloods. This was increasingly the case as they progressed deeper into the continent. At Detroit Parkman wrote in his journal about "the little squaw— the old one with her continual grin—the old man with his nose poxed away—and the rest." Weak and thin, they were drinking rum from a kettle.

From Detroit the Tjernagel party steamed through Lake Saint Clair and the river of that name into Lake Huron. As they proceeded northward along the east coast of Michigan they were usually in sight of land. In 1845

Parkman paid $7 for his passage from Detroit to Mackinaw, the same fare he had paid from Buffalo to Detroit.

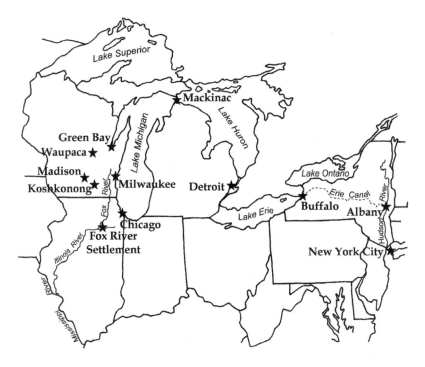

The glory days for Mackinaw at the tip of Lake Huron were over when the Tjernagels docked there in 1852. Previously, when beaver hats were in high fashion, empires and civilizations had clashed in this vicinity because lucrative fur-gathering enterprises centered their activities here with tentacles reaching hundreds of miles in every direction. Near the forty-sixth parallel, the waters of three of the Great Lakes converge. Trade routes extended back, successively, to Paris, London, and New York, depending upon the fate of nations and the treaties they negotiated. By 1852 beaver hats were out of style, trade languished, the natives were docile, and international boundaries peaceful.

Mackinaw, the farthest north Store Per reached in North America, is still fourteen degrees south of his birthplace. Here the Tjernagels likely transferred to another steamer to enter Lake Michigan through the Straits of Mackinac. Then their captain threaded a southwesterly course among islands down into Green Bay, Wisconsin.

Large steamboats burned a cord and a half of wood each hour of running time. This appetite could have provided work for the Tjernagels at any number of places between Buffalo and Green Bay. Putting up firewood was not beneath their dignity and they were efficient at such work. Perhaps they earned cash by sawing, chopping, and stacking firewood during their early weeks in America.

At Green Bay the Sveio party, now numbering about thirty (because some people siphoned off to various destinations), boarded a small river steamboat to transport them up the Fox River toward Waupaca. The number is reckoned by adding the fourteen names Endre gave to Nehemias to the composition of the Lie and Nygaard families whom Endre acknowledged being present and whose names appear in the *Rogaland* passenger list. The intent was to find Michael Lie and his wife Anna Marie who were "supposed to have located somewhere in this part of the country." All went well as the steamer bucked the current of the Fox River in a southwesterly direction into Lake Winnebago.

Accounts by Peder Gustav and Nehemias, as well as a 1941 narrative by their oldest brother, Lars Johan, all place Anna Marie's parents, Kjersteen and Phillipus, aboard the steamer on the last leg of the journey to Waupaca. This is unlikely. They had arrived in America two years earlier. It was Michael's parents, not Anna Marie's, who made the trip from Norway to Wisconsin in the party with Store Per.

As of summer 1852 Michael, Anna Marie, and daughters Dorothy and Julia were newcomers to the forest near Waupaca. Very likely, they were squatters, which status was legal under the Preemption Law of 1841. They had come north from Koshkonong, flush with enthusiasm for land just coming on the market—enthusiasm communicated prematurely to family and friends in Sveio. They were building a cabin which they hoped to complete before winter. Then Anna Marie took sick.

It was now the second week of August and water levels were low. Complications ensued for the approaching travelers when the steamboat captain attempted to navigate what both Nehemias and Peder Gustav labeled the "Winnebago River." No such stream appears on Wisconsin maps. What they meant by the term was likely the complex of rivers and lakes, including the Upper Fox River and possibly the Wolf River, leading to the Waupaca River and the town of that name. Several miles short of Waupaca fallen pine trees and shallow water halted all progress. "The captain immediately ordered all the passengers on shore, their luggage as well," related Peder Gustav. Lars Johan identified this location in general terms as: "the west shore of Green Bay out in the utter wilderness."

At this point language became a barrier to understanding. Store Per and his Norwegian-speaking compatriots understood that after unloading the boat to get through the shallows, they would reload and resume the voyage. The captain understood differently and steamed off in the direction of Green Bay. "When it dawned upon our party what the unscrupulous captain was up to, all they could say in a beseeching tone was yes, Waupaca, Wisconsin, no?" Peder Gustav editorialized: "Woe to that captain and his crew, if Big Peer could have been wafted back into that boat just for a few minutes."

In a predicament with little food, no shelter, and only their legs for transportation, the party encountered a Frenchman left behind by the fur trade, living with two Indian wives. He "understood them no better than they did him," reads Nehemias' account. They called a council and devised a plan. Store Per would remain in camp with the women, children, and the older people. Several able-bodied men would forage for food while others would search for the residence of Anna Marie and Michael Lie.

The search party "traveled all day without any signs of any civilization," wrote Lars Johan, "but towards evening they espied a hut in the edge of the timber." The door opened and out came Michael Lie. "Now I know that there is a living God," he reportedly asserted. "You came in time to help me because just now Maria died from Asiatic Cholera." Family records record the date of her death as August 12, 1852. Endre, a member of the search party, told Lars Johan that he helped bury Anna Marie and remained that night at the Lie cabin. The next day they headed back to camp along with Michael and his two little daughters.

At camp a "sorry looking group" huddled, "waiting for something to develop," recorded Peder Gustav. They did not have to wait long. Looking up river they spotted a flotilla of canoes "manned by a goodly number of Indian warriors." Store Per then remembered the "blood-curdling Indian stories he as a boy had read back home in his native country." Would they slip by without incident? No, they came ashore. While the women cried and the children bawled, a struggle raged within Store Per. His first impulse was to fight them all "if they should decide to molest his charges." This thought dissipated when he realized their numbers and saw their weapons.

It occurred to Store Per that he could "speak another universal language." He "lifted the cover of his massive immigrant chest and drew forth his violin, clapped down the cover, sat down on it, and the concert was on." First, he played a selection of "dear old Lutheran hymns." This assured the women and children "that the good Lord and his protecting angels were hovering near." The Indians moved closer, encircling the group. "Our artist now started to offer music of a lighter vein, such as folksongs, love songs and finally wound up with a rollicking 'Springe Dans.'"

A half-century later Nehemias commissioned Chicago artist Emil Biorn to paint this scene. The image is reproduced on the back cover of this book. It shows Store Per seated on his hump-backed trunk, playing his violin in the forest, surrounded by twenty-one of his countrymen. They are eyeing a group of approaching Indians, some in buckskin and feathered headdress, who have just disembarked from their canoe.

Accounts differ as to what happened next. According to Peder Gustav, when Store Per picked up the tempo "the grim visaged countenances of our Indian warriors were transformed into winning smiles." They "saw at a glance what was needed here, food and shelter, of which they generously supplied both." Lars Johan reported that the Indians began roasting venison and "brought our friends a generous helping, which to our people tasted very good." The two groups could not communicate with each other, "except through the medium of sign language. Of course, Per would tell them a story through his violin, whenever he deemed it expedient. This was a language they understood, and fully appreciated." Two days passed during the absence of the search party.

According to Nehemias, nothing resembling an August Thanksgiving occurred. The Indians came and went while "the women and children huddled together on their travelers' chests wearied and hungry, and fearful as to the outcome." The immigrants had nothing of their own to eat except "mildewed cod-fish and a few dry crusts of bread" that had come all the way from Norway.

A persistent belief among first and second generations of Tjernagels in America was that these Indians were members of the Stockbridge Munsee Band of Mohicans whose pastor, years later, was none other than the Rev. H. M. Tjernagel, Store Per's nephew. Indeed, Helge Mathias Tjernagel served Immanuel Mohican Lutheran Church near Gresham, Wisconsin, from 1918 to 1923. In the course of an April 14, 2007, interview with eighty-nine-year-old Clarence A. Chicks of that tribe and congregation, Clarence stated that it was possible, but unlikely that his people met the Tjernagel party near Waupaca. If they did, he said, "the Tjernagels were in no danger as long as they behaved." He added that his people would likely have recognized some of the hymn tunes.

Clarence explained that in the 1850s his forebears lived and dressed much like the central Wisconsin settlers of European origin and would not have been wearing feathered headdresses. Some of the Mohicans had been English-speaking Christians since the eighteenth century. The tribe, then residing at Stockbridge, Massachusetts, received a two volume 1716-1717 English Bible donated by "His Royal Highness Frederick, Prince of Wales." Clarence's forebears carried this Bible with them as they moved westward, often in poverty and disgrace. Today it resides in a case at the Arvid E. Miller Memorial Library-Museum at Bowler, Wisconsin. "Cherished from generation to generation, taken away and then returned, the Stockbridge Bible," according to Jeff Siemers, "is an extraordinary symbol of a proud and determined people, the Stockbridge-Munsee Band of Mohican Indians."

During conversations with representatives of the Tjernagel family, sprightly Clarence A. Chicks was amused by the fact that his people spoke English in 1852, while the Tjernagels did not. Also by the fact that Norwegians soak cod in lye in the preparation of *lutefisk* while his people soak corn in lye in the preparation of corn hull soup.

The Menominees were the dominant tribe near Waupaca in 1852. Julie A. Hintz of the Waupaca Historical Society thinks it likely that members of this tribe frightened the marooned Tjernagels. Another possibility is that they were Winnebagos. Regardless of tribal affiliation, the emigrants initially misinterpreted the demeanor of the native Americans they met. Yet, all came to a peaceful resolution. Accounts of the three brothers agree that Store Per restrained his fighting instincts and calmed the people under his protection until the Indians departed "as quietly as they had come."

In a couple of days the first of the scouting and foraging parties straggled back to camp with a span of oxen "hitched to some wheels made out of disks, sawed from a proper sized log to make a wheel," wrote Peder Gustav. This unwieldy *kubberulle* was on loan from a helpful settler. Then food and two or three more ox teams arrived with grieving Michael Lie driving one of them. The party loaded its possessions on the ox carts and trekked through the forest toward Waupaca.

Not only was Michael Lie's log cabin too small to accommodate the party, it was unfinished. The family they had been counting on for assistance was in dire straits, motherless, and with Julia, the younger of the two Lie girls, barely weaned. Nor was there enough room for the new arrivals in a nearby abandoned lumberman's shanty. Consequently, the men worked during a thunderstorm to construct a lean-to out of hickory saplings and Norse *aakle*—the latter being tightly woven woolen blankets, a fabric "well nigh everlasting."

In addition to Store Per's struggles with English and with his fighting instincts (restrained during the episode with the Indians), a gastric struggle raged within him. Accustomed to dark bread and fish, Store Per's digestive system rebelled against American food. He had ridden out raging storms on the high seas without consequence, but rancid bacon and foods made from white flour turned his stomach. He "suffered greatly" from a meal of pork and dumplings. His symptoms could easily have been confused with those of Asiatic cholera to which the party had been exposed. Yet, the resourceful people from Tjernagel coped.

In their telling of the story, the three brothers correctly attributed a crucial role to Anna Marie's parents. Word must have reached them at Koshkonong that their daughter's family was in dire straits. Their response was to extend aid. At age fifty-five and without a home of her own, Kjersteen offered to take the two Lie girls, her grandchildren, and raise them as her own. Michael, her grief-stricken son-in-law, accepted the offer. Regardless of whether they struck the arrangement near Waupaca or at Koshkonong several days later, Kjersteen and Phillipus parented Dorothy and Julia until they matured and set up their own households.

The question arose for the Tjernagel party, what should they do next? Given the ceaseless rain, health problems, "seemingly poor soil," and all that had transpired, *Indilandet* did not appeal to them. "To think that they had traveled many thousand miles, endured all kinds of hardship, and then to find conditions like this. This, their much dreamed of goal, where they had intended to settle down and build for themselves a home." They must go someplace "right soon" where they could earn money. No time was wasted in agreeing to go to Koshkonong, 130 miles to the south. Michael Lie had recently lived there, he knew the way, and, within the limits of their modest means, Kjersteen and Phillipus could extend help.

Michael temporarily meshed his plans with those of the immigrant party. He had a supply of shingles to sell and decided to market them at Koshkonong, east of Madison, where a building boom was in progress. The men hoisted the trunks on top of Michael's wagonload of shingles, the oxen pulled, and off they went. Endre had sold his large trunk in New York and he left his hand trunk or *skrin* on the riverbank where the steamboat captain abandoned the party. Therefore, he had little to carry. The men walked behind the wagon carrying packs that the wagon could not accommodate and the women carried the small children. According to family tradition, Store Per carried a load "big enough for a pack mule, walking barefoot so as to save his shoes."

"It was not always easy to get food on the way," Endre explained to Nehemias. "Milk was generally to be had for the asking, which was a great help." A few settlers gave them "the cold shoulder." One woman went so far as to pour milk on the ground when the travelers refused to pay her asking price. At night the party spread out their *aakla* and slept on the ground. It took a week to walk behind the ox-drawn wagon from Waupaca to Koshkonong. Upon arrival, "footsore and weary," it was at least the third week of August. For all practical purposes, the farmers in the group had lost a growing season.

Nevertheless, the flourishing Koshkonong settlement proved to be a good place for newcomers. Founded a dozen years earlier, it was one of the early Norwegian settlements in America. At West Koshkonong an octagonal, brick church that seated 800 people was just coming into use. Rich with symbolism, its architecture carried strong messages. Seven dimensions stood for the days of the week, especially the six days of creation plus the seventh day when God rested. The eighth dimension reminded all to prepare for Judgment Day. The building would have been impressive anywhere but was all the more striking in its bucolic prairie setting. Here recent arrivals lived in log cabins but many who had been on the land for a time had progressed to substantial frame houses. By dint of their labor and cash contributions, Koshkonong Lutherans now worshiped in a beautiful edifice.

Within the octagonal church on a Sunday morning, Store Per and Malene might have thought they were in Norway. Following the familiar pattern of the Bugenhagen liturgy, they confessed their sins in their native language. Then came comforting words of absolution from the Rev. A. C. Preus: "Lift up your hearts! By the authority of God and of my holy office I forgive you all your sins, in the name of the Father and of the Son and of the Holy Spirit." Store Per heard Pastor Preus preach the Word of God in Norwegian. This stirred his soul and strengthened his faith, as did blending his voice with the voices of hundreds of like-minded worshipers in singing familiar hymns. Per was moved mightily by what he experienced at Koshkonong. Wherever he would eventually settle this was the model of what he wanted in a church and he was willing to work to achieve it. First, he must make a living and take steps toward acquiring a farm.

Along with the family of Kjersteen and Phillipus (sons Knut and Peder, daughter Helga, and the two Lie girls), Store Per and Malene remained at Koshkonong "for the time being, working at odd jobs, thus eking out a living, and incidentally laying aside a few dollars preparatory for another crusade." Hiring out to Yankees forced the immigrants to learn some English and to become familiar with American tools, farm equipment, and ways. Nearby Madison, capitol city of the State of Wisconsin, provided opportunities for learning the mysteries of American government. Store Per liked the people and rolling hills of Koshkonong but, as Michael Lie had already learned, good land in that vicinity was expensive.

As they gained confidence, the families and individuals of the Tjernagel party dispersed. In time, some became wealthy. Jokum took his family to Milwaukee where he became first mate on a lake vessel. He declared his intent to become a citizen of the United States June 23, 1855, and was sworn in as a citizen February 8, 1858. He became an owner and captain of Great Lakes ships, including a widely recognized schooner, *Jennibell,* and opened a dealership in wood and coal. Jokum ceased using the Tjernagel name and for the rest of his life was known as "Captain Christenson." When he retired and returned to Norway as a tourist in 1892, a hotel owner approached him and asked, "Don't you remember me?" Jokum replied in the negative whereupon the man explained: "I worked for you, when years ago you owned Milwaukee, more or less."

Endre, only eighteen in 1852, woke up after his first night in Milwaukee, in a house from which health officials removed the bodies of two Asiatic cholera victims. Milwaukeeans blamed the immigrants for bringing the dread disease to their town. Initially, Endre booked in as a common sailor on the same ship with Jokum but farming was his goal. He drifted to the Fox River Settlement in Illinois and eventually acquired a farm in central Iowa where we shall meet him again.

"Others," according to Peder Gustav, "got work in the logging camps." Among them was Carl Magnus

Johannesen, the Swedish cooper who married Gunilde the same day that Store Per married Malene. They Americanized their names to Charles M. and Gunhild Johnson and raised nine children. With the exception of Charles' service in the Union Army during the Civil War, they lived out their lives at Winnecone, Winnebago County, Wisconsin, where Charles worked in various capacities in the wood industry.

With each passing week of temporary living arrangements, Malene's nesting instincts grew stronger; she was "expecting" in March. Before 1852 was out, she and Store Per left Koshkonong and went to the Fox River Settlement southwest of Chicago where her widowed brother Peder owned a farm. The population schedule of the 1850 United States Census for Illinois lists him as a thirty-year-old farmer and native of Norway with two children and an estate valued at $200. According to Lars Johan Tjernagel, "He was a hard working but jovial sort of a man and very kind hearted." Peder needed someone to mother his two young sons and to assume household duties. Store Per and Malene needed a place to live until they could put down roots. Both sets of interests were served when Store Per and Malene moved in with Peder. This arrangement gave Per daily opportunities to learn about American agriculture from a successful farmer.

Kjersteen and Phillipus also made the move from Koshkonong to the Fox River Settlement. With money from the sale of their Lien farm, they bought a house and lot, "also some cattle, which the father cared for while the sons [Knut and Peder] worked on farms by the month." Given the high birth rate among young couples in the Settlement, there was ample call for Kjersteen's services as midwife. March 21, 1853, was a memorable and happy day for Malene and Store Per because a healthy daughter, Helga, was born to them. Having her aunt Kjersteen present for the birth of her first child must have been reassuring to Malena.

In her book *Homes of the New World*, the Swedish traveler, Fredrika Bremer, described the log houses where her fellow Scandinavians lived in this part of Illinois as "little birds' nests floating upon the ocean." The "ocean" in this case was the awe-inspiring prairie stretching to the horizon. In nature's vast inventory Miss Bremer regarded such scenes "grander even than Niagara." In his most expansive dreams Store Per could not imagine farmland like this. He was determined to get a slice of it, complete with a "nest" for his family.

To progress toward his goal of land ownership, Store Per followed a common pattern of young men on the agricultural frontier; he "climbed the agricultural ladder." The first rung was farm laborer or hired man; second, farm operator (renter, share cropper, or some variant of tenant farmer); third, farm owner who produced primarily for his own family; and fourth, entrepreneurial farmer who owned many acres, engaged others, and produced primarily for the market.

Sketchy evidence documents Store Per's progress toward his goal of land ownership. During his short tenure at Koshkonong, he hired out to farmers. In the Fox River Settlement he soon stepped up to the second rung of the ladder and became a tenant farmer with housing, such as it was, part of the arrangement. Per likely moved Malena and Helga out of his cousin's house and under their own roof before July 1, 1852. On that date Peder Christenson married Lowray (Louise) Thompson who needed to be in charge of her own household. The wedding gave Store Per the opportunity to bring out his violin to honor the bride and groom with Old Country tunes. Kjersteen, Phillipus, and and their children were on hand to join in the celebration as were relatives of the Quam family and other kin.

The 1855 Illinois State Census pins down basic facts about these people. The names "Peter Larson" and "Peter Crestonson" appear on page 226 of the "Census of the Inhabitants of Mission Township," the second township south of the northeast corner of LaSalle County. Cleng Peerson had been right; this is prime agricultural land. The village of Norway lies near the center of the township and the Fox River forms the better part of its western boundary. The census taker recorded Store Per's household as consisting of one free white male "30 to 40" and two free white females, one in the same age bracket as the male, and the other, obviously Helga, "under 10." Actually, neither Per nor Malena had yet reached the age of thirty. The number "1" appears in the "Militia" column. Per had no reason to suspect that in a few short years many of his neighbors, likewise members of the militia, would be fighting to preserve the Union and free the slaves. $250 appears in the "Value of Live Stock" column.

The 1855 census entry for Peder Christenson indicates that this generous man had again taken people into his household. Other sources show him as a land owner and successful farmer living near the village of Norway. Destined for the top rung of the agricultural ladder, he eventually owned three farms in Illinois and one in Iowa.

According to Lars Johan, jovial Peder Christenson "was not overly religious." Lars continued, "About this time the Lutheran Church had emissaries and laymen, who claimed they were inspired, that traveled over the country trying to save souls and incidentally made an easy living." Peder was "more taken up with this class. . . than with the regular church and his family was neglected along churchly lines." Subsequently, Peder and his new wife affiliated with the Methodist Episcopal Church. How Store Per responded to religious currents and cross currents in the Fox River Settlement is the subject of the opening section of the next chapter.

Harvesting wheat, the main cash crop on the Illinois prairie in the 1850s, required backbreaking toil. In the Old Country where fields were small, laborers plentiful, and every kernel counted, farmers used short handled sickles to cut grain. The broad fields of the American prairies called for more efficient methods. A long handled scythe with a wooden "cradle" attached to catch the grain stalks became an early laborsaving device. "At each stroke or swing with cradle a section of the swath was deposited on the ground, while the implement would be jerked back for another cut." Store Per's long arms and great strength functioned well for cradling. He cut swaths ten feet wide and reportedly cradled twelve acres a day. "Per had learned to cut the grain evenly, leaving stubble of uniform height and not too close to the ground."

An equally good man was needed to follow in the wake of the cradler to gather the clusters left on the ground and tie them into bundles with long strands of straw. Nehemias once demonstrated the technique to this writer. When Ole Andreas came to the Fox River Settlement from Norway in 1856 he could not, as bundle-maker, keep up with his big brother.

A number of machines evolved before the self-binding reaper became the standard harvesting machine after the Civil War. One unusual machine was pushed, not pulled, by two teams of horses "either side of a long tongue extending backwards at the end of which sat a helmsman on very heavy wheels controlling the direction of the machine." The machine cut ten-foot swaths and laid the grain on a platform. Two men then raked the grain stalks into bundles.

When such a machine arrived in the Fox River Settlement Store Per announced that he would do the work of both men and attend to the raking by himself. In a classic contest between man and machine, Store Per overexerted himself and sustained "lasting injury." His brother who was present explained: "He thought he would be strong enough to do it alone, but got '*slet*' in the effort." *Slet* can mean "sprained, torn, or ripped," and it can also mean "worn out." Store Per had to concede that the machine, its driver known as *den skrubben* (the wolf), and four horses could cut more grain than he could rake—a rare admission of defeat by the strongman.

Following the bundlers in the field came shockers who arranged several bundles, butt ends down, into upright shocks. These stood drying in the fields until it was time to thresh.

From Old Testament times people used wooden flails to separate kernels of grain from their husks or they used oxen to "tramp it out" on a threshing floor. They performed these tasks on hills where the wind blew the chaff away. American ingenuity rose to the challenge of "threshing" and "separating" more efficiently, first by using horses to do the tramping and then by applying animal power to treadmills that whirled cylinders bristling with wooden pins inside of a box containing the mechanism. Even these primitive "threshing machines" knocked the grain out in a hurry. Greater efficiencies came with metal cylinders and pins and the addition of fans to blow away the chaff. Routing the straw and chaff through a pipe that could be aimed to build a straw stack came later as did mounting the threshing box on wheels and powering it with a steam engine.

During his short life Store Per witnessed more improvements in the harvesting and threshing of grain than did all the generations of mankind up to his time.

Only a few more facts can be established regarding Store Per and Malene's tenure in Illinois (late 1852 until spring 1857). On April 11, 1856, Malena gave birth to her second child, Christen Johan. We can count on the fact that faithful Kjersteen ushered him into the world—as she had done for his sister two years earlier and his parents back in Norway.

Proud father and successful tenant farmer in the mid 1850s, Store Per learned American ways, saved a portion of his earnings, and earmarked the money for the purchase of land.

As the population increased in the Fox River Settlement, "the demand for good land exceeded the supply and the price of land rose so sharply . . . that a spirit of unrest stirred among many members of that settlement." Word circulated that good land was available at low prices across the Mississippi in Iowa.

In preparation for farming on his own and breaking prairie sod, Store Per acquired a yoke of powerful oxen, Buck and Pride. They may have been part of the $250 valuation for livestock in the entry for Store Per in the 1855 Illinois census. By definition, an ox is a neutered male of the bovine family. Slower, steadier, and more surefooted than a horse, an ox does not require a rich diet of grain because its four stomachs can extract nutrients even from coarse grasses. Moreover, oxen are not prone to disease or sore feet. Ole Andreas described Buck and Pride as "*svart rosete.*" *Svart* being the Norwegian word for black, they were dark, perhaps reddish black. If at least partially of the Devon breed, this would have been likely. Buck and Pride could have weighed as much as a ton each.

Oxen of all breeds have minds of their own, move slowly, and require stern taskmasters. Drivers had the reputation of using foul language and cracking their whips to resound like the detonation of small firearms. Gentle Store Per derived satisfaction from breaking Buck and Pride without using a whip and working them without raising his voice. Sometimes, however, he slapped them with his bare hands "to rouse them to their task."

Chapter Six
AN EYE TO IOWA

Life is a race and giddy climbing;
Much turns on heed and sense of timing.
While you were doodling and failed to try
Perhaps your happiness passed you by.

What motivated Store Per to leave Illinois and head west to Iowa? Inexpensive land was a strong pull, but pushing forces were at work too. Per was not pleased with the religious state of affairs in the Fox River Settlement. He recognized that some of the problems of the state churches of the Scandinavian countries had spilled over to Lutheranism in the United States.

In his highly acclaimed and historically accurate novel *The Hammer of God*, Bishop Bo Giertz has a fictional Swedish clergyman summarize his duties. As of the early years of the nineteenth century, this country pastor stated that he was expected to preach about "true virtue," defined as "raising potatoes, paying taxes, and in not forgetting to buy the king's brandy." The situation did not soon improve. Bjug Harstad, grandfather of this writer who left Setesdal, Norway, for the Fox River Settlement in 1861, characterized clergymen of his native country as "generally proud, avaricious, domineering, and vain-glorious church policemen of the king, often drunkards, a lazy and negligent lot of officers in church and state."

Both in Norway and America lay preachers arose to challenge cynicism, rationalism, indifference, and cold orthodox—especially when they emanated from aristocratic clergymen. Store Per was among those who concluded that pietistic lay preachers who claimed to be addressing wrongs often created more problems. Controversies about lay preaching swirled within families, congregations, and incipient synods. As we shall see, Store Per eventually transferred his loyalty from the State Church of Norway to a Lutheran congregation in Iowa that he had a hand in founding—a church affiliated with the Norwegian Synod that shunned the extremes of pietism.

Developments unfolded as follows. The core settlers of the Fox River Settlement were Sloopers who had come to Kendall, New York, in 1825 and moved on to Illinois in the 1830s and 1840s. They were of two religious persuasions, Quakers and followers of Hans Nielsen Hauge (1771-1824), a pietistic lay preacher. Hauge did not break with the State Church of Norway nor did he emigrate. Norway's 1814 constitution did not provide for religious freedom and government officials oppressed both groups. Hauge, in fact, spent a decade in prison for lay preaching.

Neither in New York nor in Illinois did effective secular or religious leaders emerge. An 1839 observer found "the worst heathendom" in the Fox River Settlement with no church within miles. An 1841 visitor reported that the colonists at Koshkonong "are satisfied and live a quiet, happy life in good understanding with one another." At Fox River they have good land, but for the most part "are indifferent to the common good, and quarrelsome among themselves. Religion means nothing to them whatsoever; they have abandoned its principles completely."

Elling Eielsen (1804-1883), a lay preacher who broke away from the State Church of Norway, came to the United States in 1839. He worked most of the Norwegian settlements, could not gain a foothold at Koshkonong, but found fertile ground in the Fox River Settlement. A blacksmith by trade and an engaging man, he held great power over people.

Especially during the cholera years, 1849-1854, the loss of loved ones, loneliness, and depression left settlers vulnerable to his histrionics. Unbridled emotionalism in his sermons and prayers at unstructured "meetings" (as opposed to worship services), and invective against devil-inspired, gowned clergymen who chanted and followed set liturgies in steepled churches with pulpits and altars, attracted followers. Eielsen went about his revivalistic preaching without a call from a congregation.

Those who adhered to the spirit of the Lutheran Reformation criticized Eielsen and his followers on a broad front, but most basically for stressing the importance of leading a good life to the point of compromising the redemptive work of Christ. Pietism, the label for this tendency, often coupled with other emphases such as insistence upon a personal religious experience — as was common in Reformed churches. Bjug Harstad, who knew many "Ellingians" (as did Store Per), wrote that they "wore downcast faces, often uttering pious words with hopeless sighs and groanings" because they could never be sure that their deeds "were sufficient to blot out their sins or make them acceptable to God." Eielsen left people with the impression "that the Lord is a stern judge, and that forgiveness of sin and final salvation depended on our own efforts."

Store Per could see that the Lutheranism he had known in his confirmation classes at Moster Church and had witnessed at Koshkonong was not thriving in the Fox River Settlement. He rejected his neighbor and brother-in-law Peder Christenson's response to the confused state of affairs, successively, by indifference, by coming under the influence of pietistic lay preachers, and finally by joining the Methodist Episcopal Church. Other Tjernagel relatives who went by the name of Quam in America also turned to Methodism.

Yet, there was hope for those who longed for Lutheran orthodoxy and orderly worship. Store Per and others of this mind pinned their hopes to a Lisbon, Illinois, schoolteacher and native of Stavanger, Peter Andreas Rasmussen (1829-1898). Once an Eielsen follower, Rasmussen went off to the Lutheran Church, Missouri Synod's practical theological seminary at Fort Wayne, Indiana, and returned as an ordained clergyman in 1854. He opened a short-lived seminary at Lisbon and set his students to memorizing the entire Augsburg Confession of 1530. Article XIV of the document helps to explain why he changed his position regarding lay preaching and Elling Eielsen: "Of ecclesiastical order we teach that no one should publicly teach in the church or administer the sacraments unless he is rightfully called." Until he was ordained, called, and installed (all of which eventually did take place), Eielsen stood in violation of basic Lutheran tenets about church and ministry.

Bjug Harstad, confirmed by Pastor Rasmussen in 1863 and later a Norwegian Synod pastor, noted that the Fox River Settlement became "a dumping grounds for all kinds of Norwegian religious vagabond spirits" including infidels, scoffers, pietists, lay preachers, and members of sects. As of the mid 1850s, Store Per grasped this trend and concluded that this was not a good place to raise his family. In the habit of reading his Bible when perplexed, he would have found pertinence in St. Paul's letter to the Ephesian Christians (4:13-14) to become mature in the faith. "Then we will no longer be infants, tossed back and forth by the waves, and blown here and there by every wind of teaching and the craftiness of men in their deceitful scheming. Instead, speaking the truth in love, we will in all things grow up into him who is the Head, that is, Christ."

Store Per resolved to do just that. He soon found himself in planning and leadership roles among people who were ready to leave an Illinois *humlebol* (hornet's nest), as one called it. The plan that began to unfold involved like-minded families moving to the Iowa frontier, acquiring land, and taking advantage of an offer from Pastor

Rasmussen to help found churches west of the Mississippi that would be faithful to God's Word.

The concept had precedent in America going back to 1620. The Mayflower Compact asserts that the Pilgrims came to Plymouth, Massachusetts, "for ye glorie of God and advancement of ye Christian faith." In the eighteenth century entire congregations moved from the southern uplands, over the mountains, and into the backcountry where the rivers flowed westward. In the Fox River Settlement in the mid 1850s, a group of cautious people with an eye to Iowa began to coalesce. Before establishing specific plans, they would dispatch an advance party to check localities and bring back recommendations.

Accordingly, in the summer of 1856 a delegation of land-hungry Norwegian-Americans, mostly natives of Sveio, some with Tjernagel blood in their veins, turned to men they trusted. They chose Store Per and his friend from youth, *Taalige* Lars Henderson, to "spy out the land" across the river. In March that year Lars had left Norway for good, this time with his wife Anna, and three children under the age of five.

Anxious to acquire good farmland for themselves and the people who dispatched them, the two family men knew what to look for. They had the skills to analyze locations and soils and the maturity to make recommendations based on facts and good judgment. Their peers recognized this, as well as Store Per's capacity for leadership. Were Per and friends to "settle" on the Iowa frontier, all knew that survival must be the first order of business. Then they could turn to church matters.

No evidence of a written "compact" among the eventual migrants has surfaced, nor is there testimony from Store Per gauging the extent to which religious issues determined the decision about moving west. However, the chronicler of Per's two treks to Iowa (to be quoted shortly) left little doubt that religious matters did play a

role. Near the close of Chapter 9, Rev. Rasmussen's role in helping lay leaders, Store Per among them, establish a church at Story City is detailed.

The chronicler of both the 1856 and 1857 expeditions, Erik Arnesen Travaas, described Per as "a very gigantic figure" reminiscent of "an old Norwegian giant with steel in arm setting out on a Viking expedition." Although Store Per was talkative and good-natured, it was unwise to earn his disfavor. "Then a bear hug would be much more preferred than a hug with him."

In contrast, Lars, a small, thoughtful, diffident gentleman said little "except in private to his favorite ox-team." At home and abroad his loquacious wife Anna did the talking for the family. Lars Johan Tjernagel remembered her restless tongue and curly black hair that bobbed as she walked from cabin to cabin while knitting. He agreed with Travaas: "'Taalige' Lars was a quiet man without any bluff or bluster," then added "but knew just what he wanted." In the Fox River Settlement his descriptive nickname distinguished him from another man, also married to an Anna, who sometimes went by the name Lars Henderson and at other times Lars Henryson. Born at Etne, Norway, he had come to America aboard the *Kong Sverre* in 1847 along with his twin brother Torkel who consistently used the name Henryson. Both Lars Hendersons had an eye to Iowa; both weave in and out of the remainder of our story.

Writing in 1888, Travaas presented basic facts, but also gave wide berth to his imagination. He may have been the first writer to portray a larger-than-life Store Per.

The 1856 reconnaissance began with Per whistling an old tune while contemplating the stony fields back in Norway. From early childhood in their native land the two scouts had "gotten in the habit of waiting for everything with patience . . . . A trip over the wild prairie demands patience like nothing else."

The twosome crossed the Mississippi River at Davenport. Ralph Waldo Emerson, the New England intellectual, had entered Iowa through this gateway a few months earlier while on the lecture circuit. He captured the spirit of the times with a journal entry at the Le Claire House where he stayed December 31, 1855. Land fever was so pervasive, he wrote, that it dominated everyday speech. "They talk 'quarter-sections.'" Emerson overheard one man order a quarter-section of pie.

When Lars and Per reached the border of Story County in central Iowa, then populated with only 2,868 people, the wild prairie began to show its vastness. Although they were in the middle of a continent the "endless plains" appeared to the two Norwegians as "a troubled sea where the waves begin to subside after a storm." They were not alone with this observation. "Look around in every quarter of the compass," wrote a British sea captain, "not a landmark, not a vestige of any thing human but yourself. Instead of sky and water, it is one vast field, bounded only by the horizon, its surface gently undulating like the waves of the ocean; and as the wind (which always blows fresh on the prairies) bows down the heads of the high grass, it gives you the idea of a running swell."

After the scouts gained their composure "They were very surprised about all the uncultivated land which lay here waiting to be changed to productive acres and meadows." Enthused and out of range of his wife's incessant talking, *Taalige* Lars began to patter: "'Just look . . . . Here it's possible to get yourself a very large farm'. . . . Per thought the same way. 'And just imagine how we can reap with longhandled scythes,' continued Lars. 'It will certainly be better than puttering along with a shorthandled sickle and cutting every little straw among the stones as we had to do back home.' 'Yes', said Per and laughed a little."

The evening prior to their arrival at Nevada (the first "a" is long), Travaas has Store Per imagine "the beautiful settlement that the Norwegian settlers, in a short time, would establish in this country." He thought "how nice it would be when they could come so far that they could together build a church, call a pastor, and have it just like it was at home where they could go to church and hear God's word, hear the lovely old hymn tunes that could, so wonderfully dispose one to devotion and holy sadness."

Thus Travaas linked Per with the interpretation set forth at the outset of this chapter. Travaas also linked Per with a now-accepted broad interpretation that many Norwegians came to America in the nineteenth century not to break with the past but to preserve a way of life they had little chance of maintaining in the Old Country. More often than not, that life centered on agriculture. In the realm of religion, at least for Per, it entailed yearnings for a church with the same doctrine, liturgy, and music as the State Church of Norway, but without the tie to government. "In some ways we are more Norwegian here than they are in Norway," wrote a Norwegian-born editor of his countrymen nestled in rural communities in the American Midwest.

At Nevada Per and Lars observed a cluster of log structures and the beginnings of a county seat town that overly optimistic promoters touted as the next capital of the State of Iowa. After all, Iowa City, the capital since territorial days, was too far east of the center of the state and Fort Des Moines was too far south. Town promoters and farmers were not the only people who saw potential at Nevada. As the national economy boomed, lawyers, surveyors, land agents, and speculators swarmed with a frenzy that filled the *Nevada Directory For 1857* with the names of plungers. One of the enthusiasts told Per and Lars that if they set a course toward the north and west they would find "all the land they wished to inspect" and fewer people. At the future site of Roland "they began to look around really well." Here deep soil nourished lush prairie vegetation.

Farmers harbored mixed feelings about prairies and prairie plants. By all standards they were beautiful, especially in the spring and early summer. Leaves of the magical compass plant pointed north and south, which helped observant travelers keep their bearings when the sun was obscured. Such grasses as big blue stem, tall as a man on the back of a horse, provided nutritious forage any time of the year. On the negative side, the deep, tangled roots of the prairie plants yielded reluctantly to the plow. Two or more teams of oxen were sometimes needed to break the sod.

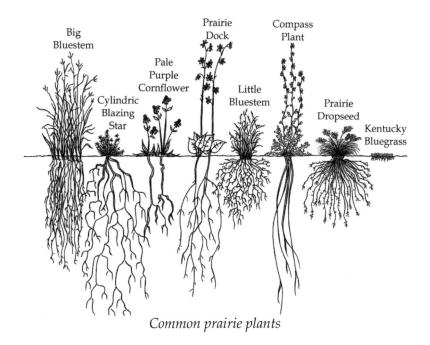

Common prairie plants

More ominous, each autumn tons of dried plant material per acre provided tinder for all-consuming, fast-moving prairie fires. Those already on the land knew the dangers. James Sowers who came to central Iowa from Lafayette, Indiana, in 1854 explained: "The greatest fires came from the northwest and fed on the heavy grass of prairie stretching without interruption all the way from the Boone River and southeast to the Skunk." Sowers had witnessed flames "high as a house" advancing at "race-horse speed" sweeping everything before them. "It was a thrilling, awe-inspiring sight." Whether ignited by lightning or careless people, fires threatened lives and property until farmers could break up the contiguous prairie. Some guide books advised against buying land on the open prairie. Property on the margin near a river might be safe, but only if settlers plowed circles around their farmsteads and controlled the tinder between the furrows with periodic "backfires."

Such considerations engaged the minds of the two land cruisers. "If they could just find some wood for fuel, for building a house and such," the land they were looking at would be ideal. A man directed them five or six miles further west where they reached "the splendid woods along the Skunk River." Originally known as the Chicaque, the pioneers renamed it the Skunk, reportedly because of the abundant population of that animal and, allegedly, because of the stream's tendency to wander through the land "oozing objectionable liquid." Rumors circulated that the land is particularly fertile where skunks abound.

Travaas did not mention that in 1856 a sprinkling of Norwegians from the Fox River Settlement was already at work building cabins and establishing farms in northwest Story County near the Skunk River and the newly platted town of Fairview. That town failed to materialize but eventually metamorphosed into Story City. These people, by and large, were not from Sveio and had their own dynamics. Per and Lars pressed on. They wanted both higher ground and ample acres for relatives and like-minded settlers in months and years to come.

Iowa maps of 1856 show a large Webster County north and west of Story County and due north of Boone County. Iowa's political leaders were then planning to impose a greater degree of order upon central Iowa. In a matter of months, the General Assembly organized

Hamilton County with its present boundaries and Webster City as its county seat.

As Per and Lars proceeded northward from the Fairview town site on the east side of Skunk River they came to hills in what is now Scott Township that undulated above the surrounding wetlands. "The sight of the rolling prairies of this township must have been a cause of joy to the settler who had been dragging his westward course through swamps and sloughs in search of the promised land," wrote a Hamilton County historian in 1912.

Here settlers could build cabins on dry land and begin farming immediately without digging drainage ditches. Nearby, Per and Lars observed "the richness of the woods which in the future would be of much benefit." Store Per thanked providence for bringing them "to this fertile land whose richness, by diligence and work," he prophesied, "will be inherited from generation to generation." In their enthusiasm, Per and Lars may not have realized that they had crossed the northern boundary of Story County and were in the southernmost reaches of Hamilton County.

A bonus of the locality was the presence of a natural feature that seemed to defy the law of gravity. In certain places, even near the crests of hills, fresh water rises to the surface. "Flows" Iowans call them. Geologists explain that underground watercourses whose faraway sources are higher than any observable feature of the landscape follow the curvature of the underlying layers of rock. Water flows to the surface where it finds openings—in some places with considerable force.

Store Per had learned about squatting from Michael Lie near Waupaca in 1852 and about "proving up" and acquiring title from farmers at Koshkonong and the Fox River Settlement. Whether he took initial steps during the 1856 reconnaissance to acquire the specific parcel he would settle upon the next spring, section thirty-three of what is now Scott Township, is unknown. For a time it was known as Norway Township and was so designated in the 1860 United States Census.

Satisfied that this area "would be best suited for beginning a Norwegian settlement" the scouts returned to Illinois. "With liveliness and confidence," *Taalige* Lars and Store Per gathered the interested parties and told them about the fertile land they had seen, "about the beautiful woods that grew by the Skunk River, and about the gigantic prairie grass that stood like a little forest and waved in the wind." They reported no Philistines inhabiting the area, only docile Indians who occasionally fished the Skunk River but lived elsewhere. They had found the Promised Land. "When they were through telling [about] it, all went home."

The time had come for interested families to take stock. They knew the economic realities. As Erik and Tor Saevereid wrote to relatives back in Norway, "Land is expensive in Illinois: 8-20 dollars per acre. But in Iowa the price is 1 ¼ dollars." To "build up a farm," the Saevereids reported that a man needed:

> 2 horses about 300 dollars
> or 2 oxen about 100 dollars
> a cow about 80 dollars
> a plow about 12-14 dollars.

In addition, a man needed about $100 for a sturdy wagon for moving his family to Iowa. Thereafter, it could serve as a farm wagon. If a family had Illinois land to sell, the money could be applied to expenses.

That winter planning began for a spring departure. Meetings resolved such issues as the date of departure, organization of the wagon train, daily schedules, security, discipline, and functions of various people. For example, some young men were designated cattle drovers.

Store Per's brother, Ole Andreas, recorded these preparations for his trip from the Fox River Settlement to Iowa a few years later. For $110 he purchased a sturdy "patent skein wagon with screw nut" suitable for farm work. It had a spring seat and a six-inch top box upon which he painted eight blue roses. At a "dear" price, he engaged a blacksmith to make iron clamps which he fastened, inside the box. Into these he inserted wooden "schooner hoops" over which he stretched four widths of muslin. The muslin repelled drops of rain, even torrents, but did not keep fine mist out of the wagon. Wealthier travelers covered the muslin with oilcloth. Ole Andreas stashed $400 into his load, but these were inflated Civil War dollars. His big brother's dollars were likely fewer, but more valuable.

When spring arrived in 1857, sixteen families (named in the notes for this chapter) totaling about eighty people, and a train of about sixteen wagons rigged as prairie schooners moved out for the 300-mile trip to central Iowa. In the lead was "the finest ox team that ever came out of the Fox River Settlement," Buck and Pride. Store

Per was reportedly the only man in the train who did not carry an ox whip. In his covered wagon were Malene, four-year-old Helga, and year-old Christen Johan. Close by in their rig were *Taalige* Lars, his wife Anna, and their three children, all under the age of five. Again, one of Malene's half brothers, Anders Christenson from Tjernagel South (not to be confused with Endre who was still sailing the Great Lakes and came to Iowa later), joined the party.

From well-packed wagons "Norwegian trunks, with their large strange *rosemaling*" (rose painting) peeked out into the sunlight. These sturdy containers that had crossed the Atlantic protected "their most holy treasures"—the Bible, the hymnbook received at confirmation, and love gifts "that dear hands had given" upon departure from Norway.

The cavalcade moved slowly across Illinois not only because families hauled their household goods, plows, tools, and poultry, but also because the procession included cattle, all too inclined to graze their way westward—despite the prodding of the drovers. There were eggs to eat, chickens to roast, milk to drink, and occasionally a calf to slaughter for veal. Each morning the travelers poured surplus milk into jugs and hung them from the ribs of the schooner top; "by evening the swaying of the moving vehicles had transformed the contents into butter and buttermilk." As during the Atlantic crossing, Sundays were devoted to worship, rest, and recreation.

Details from a wagon train that made the same trek a year earlier indicate that such trips should not be thought of as pleasure excursions: "At one point the caravan halted for a few days because a river was in flood" and could not be forded. "Once the caravan remained in camp for an extra day to bury one of the men who had suffered cramps while swimming and was drowned. One birth was recorded; both mother and infant were able to travel the following day."

One of the drovers, Stone Charlson, related to Nehemias that the 1857 caravan crossed the Mississippi River at Davenport "on a large ferry carrying passengers, wagons and teams, their cattle, and all." As they neared the Iowa shore "a cow grew restless . . . and leapt overboard." This threw the men into consternation as to how to rescue her. While they debated the merits of ropes and tackle versus boats and hooks, Store Per "acted quietly and effectively by reaching out and catching the bewildered creature by the horns and, kneeling, drew her bodily from the water onto the ferry. He said nothing, nor did the astounded lookers-on." Nehemias added: "So much for unusual strength combined with calm judgment."

All went well as the wagons rolled westward about fifteen miles per day. When darkness fell, according to Travaas, the party encamped and "all sit in an intimate circle and talk until far into the night." The men took turns with sentry duty. Good planning, communication, leadership, and good fortune resulted in a successful journey. The trip across the western half of Illinois and the eastern half of Iowa took about twenty days—busy days for Malene and Anna Henderson who had small children in tow.

Years later Malene told stories to her grandchildren about how her large, powerful, and competent husband pushed "stuck wagons" out of the mud as they crossed streams on the way to their new homes in Iowa.

Chapter Seven

A PRAIRIE HOME

There were giants in the earth in those days.

"Peter Larson," *Taalige* Lars Henderson, and their party arrived in Scott Township "early in 1857," recorded J. W. Lee in his 1912 *History of Hamilton County, Iowa.* One option for them was to claim land under terms of the Preemption Law of 1841. The intent of this law was to convey land to people who would farm it rather than to land speculators. Surveyors had already divided the township into thirty-six sections one mile square, each consisting of 640 acres.

The Preemption Law allowed settlers to file claims at the United States Land Office at Fort Dodge for a maximum of 160 acres (a quarter section), or a minimum of eighty acres of public domain. It required them to occupy the land for six months, improve it, and then pay $1.25 per acre for it. The initial filing and the final "proving up" required trips to the Land Office. Upon satisfying requirements, attending to paperwork, and paying the fees, "original entrymen" received land patents signed by the President of the United States. With these documents in hand, owners could file deeds for their property in the Hamilton County Courthouse in Webster City.

Acquiring land in this way required knowledge of the law, travel, and attention to detail. The Land Office had opened for business at the Commissary Building at Fort Dodge November 5, 1855. As the crow flies, it is over

127

forty miles to the northwest of Norway Township. Webster City is on the way to Fort Dodge but because of timing it was seldom possible to combine trips to the Land Office and the courthouse. Few newcomers to America could handle the legalities of acquiring land without assistance.

Torkel Henryson and his twin brother Lars mastered the intricacies of American land law and lent assistance to their countrymen, but neither was on hand when members of the 1857 party needed help. Nor had the Norwegians of Hamilton County yet organized claims clubs to protect themselves from men who jumped claims or used complicated laws to outmaneuver naïve settlers. Major William Williams of the United States Army, an eyewitness of skullduggery at the Fort Dodge Land Office, minced no words when he recorded "attacks" upon settlers by an "unprincipled set of pirates."

Exactly when and how Store Per and *Taalige* Lars initiated the process of acquiring title to adjoining properties in section thirty-three is uncertain. Those who settled on the public domain, built cabins, and began farming before securing title were "squatters." Squatting was not illegal. In fact the Preemption Law protected the interests of squatters. However, neither Store Per nor his friend moved decisively enough to avail themselves of these protections.

Alpha G. Person, a Yankee land speculator, outmaneuvered the two Norwegians. Title searches, abstracts, and documents in the Hamilton and Story County Courthouses reveal how he did it.

Person was the "original entryman" on the northeast quarter of the northwest quarter of section thirty-three — forty acres of well-drained land acquired, "fair and square," from the federal government on April 17, 1856. As the economy boomed, it appears that Person planned to use this parcel as a base for contiguous acquisitions, and then sell the land at a markup. It is unlikely that Person was present when the two scouts reconnoitered in 1856 or when they settled the next spring. Person's forty lay due east of the parcel Store Per settled upon and adjoined it. This forty was integral to Lars' interests. (After it passed through the hands of another owner Lars eventually bought it and added it to his core holdings.)

Person thwarted the interests of Per and Lars by playing a trump card — a land warrant granted for military service. Despite the fact that he did not perform that service, Person acted within the letter of the law when he used the warrant to acquire title to the land upon which the two Norwegians were apparently squatting.

The United States government issued the warrant under an Act of Congress of February 11, 1847, "to raise for a limited time an additional military force" for service during the Mexican War. Hiram Carr, "a Sergeant afterwards promoted to a Lieutenant in Captain Danlys Company Arkansas Volunteers," received warrant # 78243, but died without redeeming it. The administrator of Carr's estate sold the warrant which surfaced in Iowa in the possession of Alpha G. Person, a teamster and native of Vermont turned small-time land speculator. The 1856 Iowa State Census identifies him as a thirty-year-old male living in Story County.

On April 1, 1858, Person used the 1847 warrant issued to Carr to acquire "the North West quarter of Section thirty-three, in Township Eighty-six North, of Range Twenty-three West, in the district of Lands subject to sale at Fort Dodge, Iowa." This description includes the land that became Store Per's farm and some of the land that became *Taalige* Lars' farm. The presumption is that the two Norwegians squatted on these acres during their first year in Iowa.

The military land warrant trumped measures Per and Lars may have taken toward acquiring title. As of April 1, 1858, they had not "proved up" on their claims. Nor had they successfully invoked terms of the Preemption Law or the rules of any claims club to protect their interests. Short of walking away from a year's work, they had no other choice than to come to terms with Person.

Store Per's temper certainly flared when he realized this, but his spirit was not broken.

The record shows that "Peter Larson" paid Alpha G. Person $3 per acre (a total of $160) for fifty-three and one-third acres in section thirty-three and filed the deed in the Hamilton County Courthouse October 6, 1858. The same transaction extinguished Lucy Person's dower rights to the property. Lars' transaction with Person is identical in timing and price. He and Per acted in consort to reach the third rung of the agricultural ladder on the same day. Had they been able to buy the land directly from the federal government the price would have been $1.25 per acre.

Had not a speculative bubble burst several months earlier, the price of the land would have been much higher. Chastened by a slowed economy following the Panic of 1857, Person turned away from land speculation. The 1860 federal census shows him as a farmer in Palestine Township of Story County with Lucy and two boys in his household.

As of October 6, 1858, the two friends held clear title to land that had come to the United States as part of the Louisiana Purchase of 1803. Indian title had been extinguished. Their farms, small by modern standards, were several times larger than their fathers' holdings back in Norway, and the soil was much better. There were no medieval encumbrances or rents to pay nor any laws favoring the interests of a firstborn son in the disposition of the property.

A sequel to Store Per's land transaction came fifty years later on May 2, 1908, when a subsequent landowner filed a corrective deed in the Hamilton County Recorder's Office including a copy of Person's 1858 patent bearing the signature of President James Buchanan.

Two natural features that initially attracted Store Per to section thirty-three sustained him through his land title difficulties — a hill as high above the surrounding wetlands as a "crow's nest" above the deck of a schooner, and a "flow" just below the crest of the west-facing slope of the property.

Per's goal for 1857, his first year on the land, was to "settle" early enough in the season to plow some furrows, plant "sod corn" and potatoes, and help Malene scratch some garden seeds into the soil. By the onset of cold weather he must provide secure housing. During their early weeks on the land we can imagine Store Per and his family, along with the Hendersons, living out of their prairie schooners near their source of water while gathering material for the construction of a dwelling. The cattle could graze the open prairie until winter, but the cows that provided sustenance for the children must be rounded up and milked each morning and evening. Before the day of wire fences, pioneers depended upon their dogs to keep pigs, chickens, and other animals away from tender crops.

The only building materials for a cabin on section thirty-three were stone for the foundation and sod for the roof. Trees did not grow there. A tall grass prairie is not a receptive environment for the germination of tree seedlings. If any did get started periodic prairie fires destroyed them. Therefore Store Per acquired rights (and later title) to a woodlot in section thirty-one of Norway

Township. Its section lines cross the Skunk River where valuable stands of oak, hickory, black walnut, and cherry lined the meandering stream (and still do). From his camp Store Per could see his woodlot two miles west and one-quarter mile south. While Malene tended the children he spent many days felling trees and "gee-hawing" Buck and Pride across the prairie with loads of logs for his cabin.

The old pioneers "had an eye for fine locations," reported Nehemias Tjernagel. This penchant he attributed to their desire for "home and happiness." Per's thoughts must have progressed as follows: "The best vistas on my property are toward the west and south in the direction of my woodlot, Skunk River, the Fairview town site, and Long Dick Creek. I will ignore the cardinal points of the compass and take advantage of the prairie panorama by facing our cabin in a south westerly direction." Thus he sited the cabin on the hill a quarter mile back from the western boundary of his property, well above the mosquito-infested wetlands, and close to the source of potable water, the flow. "Malene will be pleased that water will be a few feet from the cabin door," he reasoned, "I shall indulge my sailor's eye for the horizon, and the family will breathe fresh prairie zephyrs on hot summer days."

Using rocks left by the last glacier, Store Per stubbed the foundation for the cabin, measuring perhaps twelve by fourteen feet, into the hillside. After he squared and notched his logs, he summoned help to raise them into position.

While en route to Iowa the sixteen families, some of them blood relatives from Sveio, had pledged to help one another with the heavy work. Now they responded to each other's calls and came together for cabin raisings along with other neighbors. These were joyful, lively events. As the men tested their strength muscling heavy logs into place, they chewed tobacco, cursed the land sharks, shared farming experiences, talked politics, and learned from experienced craftsmen. The women could not escape child-tending responsibilities, but they interrupted their routines of domestic toil with a welcome day of visiting and food sharing.

Because of his strength, skill, musical talents, and good humor, Store Per received hearty welcomes on these occasions. He and *Taalige* Lars likely helped a neighbor build a log cabin that is incorporated into a farmhouse that still stands on the "Anfenson place" one mile west of their property in section thirty-two. The logs are squared and straight, the joints tightly fitted, and the interstices carefully chinked—a record of Norwegian-American craftsmanship of the 1850s and a tribute to it.

With the logs raised, openings cut for windows and a door, and with the ridgepole in place, the mood at house raisings shifted from work to celebration. Pietistic Haugeaners and followers of Elling Eielsen then excused themselves and headed home. They knew that many work crews followed a Norwegian custom of dousing the ridgepole with spirituous liquor. Then it was time to tune up the fiddles, pass the jug, and dance the night away. If Yankee fiddlers were present their tunes mingled with Store Per's repertoire of melodies from Hordaland. On occasions when Yankee musicians predominated, the

Norwegians tired of endless repetitions of *Turkey in the Straw* and *The Road to California*. Nevertheless, people came away from cabin bees with spirits renewed and news to discuss for days. On occasion, a young man went home with a black eye.

After a cabin bee it became the owner's responsibility to ready the structure for occupancy by completing construction of the roof. Standard materials on the prairie were brush, sod, and marsh grass. Store Per and all others who attempted to fabricate watertight roofs from such materials found the task daunting. One exasperated couple removed the hoops and canopy from their prairie schooner, brought the apparatus inside their leaky cabin, and installed it over their bed. Prolonged rains motivated pioneer women to place containers in strategic places in their cabins to catch the drips.

For a time, a dirt floor would have to do; inevitably there would be critters. Malene and Anna Henderson struggled to keep their toddlers sanitary. The Norwegians learned tricks from the Yankees to make their cabins comfortable and attractive. They filled the large spaces between logs with "kneaded soil" and whitewashed the interiors. With proper chinking and a Franklin stove or a hearth, even crude cabins could be "snug and warm as you please." According to Peder Gustav, Store Per completed his log cabin "inside of an incredible short time."

Household furniture was mostly hand-made, chairs (*krak* in the vernacular) "being fashioned from hollow logs sawed through lengthwise, with saplings for legs." *Aaklar* spread out on the floor served as beds until better alternatives, "preferably with legs," could be made or purchased. Cord beds with straw mattresses became the norm. Store Per would need a strong one. With ropes strung tightly and mattresses patted into shape, sleep came quickly to those who toiled on the prairie. The expression "sleep tight" entered the vocabulary during the era of rope beds. When a better day dawned, it would not be difficult to move out of a small cabin with a dirt floor into a spacious frame house with a shingled roof.

While Store Per and his neighbors were building their cabins, setting up households, and breaking prairie sod, economic and political storm clouds gathered over Iowa and the nation. Late in the summer of 1857 overinvestment in railroads and a spirit of intense speculation led to panic in the nation's financial centers followed by depression. January 13, 1858, Iowa's first governor under a new state constitution, Republican Ralph P. Lowe, lamented in his inaugural address: "all business transactions have certainly been deranged; the commercial sky overclouded, the whole country smitten as with a palsy, and this period marked as one of uncommon solemnity." Governor Lowe attributed a troubling political situation to the United States Supreme Court's Dred Scott decision and Democratic President James Buchanan's mishandling of issues related to the institution of slavery in Kansas. He hoped that Iowans would "never consent that this state shall become an integral part of a 'great slave republic.'" Freedom-loving Norwegians agreed.

It is unlikely that Store Per yet comprehended the economic and political complexities of his adopted country or participated in protest meetings such as the one held February 6, 1858, a few townships to the south in Story County "for the purpose of organizing a protective committee to prevent the sacrifice of property at sheriff and constable sales." But he did understand his obligations. Depression notwithstanding, he paid off Alpha G. Person, as previously stated, and held clear title to his farm as of October 6, 1858.

None of Store Per's initial buildings survive. Nevertheless, one can "read like a palimpsest" the farmstead that has evolved on his property and speculate about how developments unfolded there. After completion of his cabin, Store Per's second building was likely an animal shed or log barn tucked into the hillside to the south and east of his cabin. Other such buildings in the locality had doors strong enough to confine valuable animals and roofs of brush and slough hay. A deteriorating 1884 barn measuring 104 feet by 64 feet presently stands downhill from the cabin and stable sites, situated to take advantage of a gravity flow water system originating at the artesian well. The flow, deliberately plugged when no longer needed to water livestock, broke loose December 26, 2008, and formed a pool behind the restored 1874 farmhouse. Nature will have its way.

The house defies Iowa's foursquare correctness. A logical explanation is that it mimics the angle of Store Per's cabin that stood on or near the site, and for the same reason—it offers a commanding view of the prairie.

When the present owner excavated to rebuild a kitchen porch at the back of the house in 1996, he unearthed metal artifacts from the pioneer period. Among them are a rustic drawer pull and tools for tending a hearth or large stove that predated the 1874 house. They were lost or cast aside when the cabin came down. According to Darrell Henning, an expert on Iowa's log structures, twenty years was a good life span for a log cabin. As a dwelling, Store Per's apparently lasted seventeen. Often, such buildings were put to adaptive uses. A log corncrib on high ground likely completed the first generation of buildings on the farmstead.

Store Per's farm predated all county roads in the area. From the north/south road that now defines the western border of section thirty-three, a quarter-mile-long lane curves up the hill toward the house. The lane orients the farmstead toward the Skunk River woods and Story City, not toward Randall or Roland which are closer, but did not exist when Store Per laid his plans. A row of cottonwood trees with growth rings dating back to his day forms a windbreak on the north side of the lane. Store Per must have planted them.

One more vestige of Store Per's planning brings us back poignantly to 1857—a cemetery on high ground northwest of the house. Older people in the community report that a thoughtless headstone cutter removed and recycled the gravestones in the 1940s. The present owner counts at least seven irregularly spaced depressions of varying sizes which he believes are the graves of as many individuals.

Chances are that one of the smaller graves is that of Store Per and Malene's second child, Christen Johan. Born April 11, 1856, he died May 28, 1857. No place of burial or cause of death appears in family records. Searches for his grave in cemeteries in the Fox River Settlement have come up negative, as have searches of other cemeteries near his parents' new home in Iowa. He must have died close to the time of the family's arrival in Hamilton County. As yet there was no Lutheran church or resident pastor to serve the spiritual needs of the Peder Larson Tjernagel family. The head of the household would take measures to remedy that.

A lone pine stands sentinel on the northern edge of the abandoned family cemetery near the northwest corner of section thirty-three of what was once Norway Township. It did not grow there by chance.

In Scandinavia people buried their dead in consecrated ground near churches. Farmsteads were clusters of buildings, often accommodating multiple families, as was the case at Lien and the two Tjernagel farms. It was different in Iowa. When Store Per paused to reflect after he had settled on his own land, his thoughts might have paralleled those of the Swedish traveler Fredrika Bremer: "How grand is the impression produced by this infinite expanse of plain, with its solitude and its silence!"

For Malene the solitude and silence were sometimes anything but grand. As we shall see, things came to the breaking point for her in 1863. Nevertheless, when trouble came to one settler, others would lend assistance, "and thus a very close bond among the new settlers was established and somehow the community managed to get along satisfactorily."

Anna Henderson, a catalyst for communication in the new community, reportedly walked from cabin to cabin, arriving just in time for coffee. After she died *Taalige* Lars' second wife, another Anna, carried on in the same tradition. On one occasion when Store Per's sister-in-law, Martha Karina, offered her fresh spring water "she squinted in the direction of the coffee urn and said: 'I do not thole water.'" When she got what she wanted "she went smiling on her way with the aroma of her favorite beverage clinging to her like a garment."

Before the advent of towns and railroads in central Iowa the pioneers "drove to Iowa City, 150 miles distant, to obtain clothing, salt, flour and other provisions," reported Rasmus Sheldall. "They wore wooden and rawhide shoes and subsisted largely on hominy and pork, corn mush and milk." The pioneers supplemented this diet with whatever they could glean from the land or catch in nearby streams. The prairie was destined to change. "The prairie chickens, which had enjoyed peace and quiet for many years, cackled and courted each other in the tall prairie grass," wrote Erik Arnesen Travaas. "They could not understand what all this commotion should mean. Wandering, they stood and looked at the man behind the plow" and occasionally interrupted the monotony of his diet.

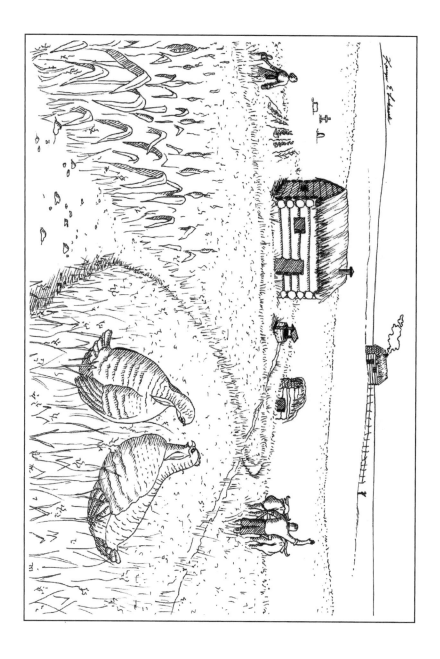

In his idealized account Travaas portrayed Store Per and Malene as newlyweds when they arrived in Iowa. Actually, they had been married five years and Malene had given birth to two children, the younger of whom had died in the spring of 1857. Nevertheless, Travaas continued his word picture of big and broad-shouldered Store Per breaking sod on his own land with his own plow, pulled by his own oxen, "with an expression on his face that witnesses to joy and inner happiness." This is why he had come to America. "He takes long thoughtful steps and shouts now and then, a haw and gee to . . . [Buck and Pride] who obediently must go according to his thundering voice." On a hill nearby "stands his new log house, really quite simple, but inside is Per's sweet girl. Like the friendly sun in May, she goes here, spreading sunshine and coziness for her good Per."

"A little ways off we see another new log house," continued Travaas. "Here we find Lars with his beloved wife. Both seem to be glad and happy." In reality the Hendersons too experienced loss. In May 1860, Anna gave birth to a baby girl, Ann, who died at the age of eight days, cause "unknown," according to the Mortality Schedule of the United States Census of that year. Tragedy struck again when her oldest brother, Helge, died of consumption and was buried beside his little sister "in a private burying-ground near the old home." This may be the cemetery on Store Per's adjoining property. "Lars lovingly tended the little graveyard while he lived, but later when the farm was sold, the new owner . . . put his plow to it," lamented Nehemias Tjernagel.

In contrast to Travaas' glowing account, Nehemias emphasized the harshness and hard work of pioneering. Sweating plowmen and straining beasts taxed their energy to the limit to prepare the prairie for crops. "Nature had entrenched its plant-root network in the ground so firmly that it took much power and finely tempered implements to lay open and reverse its rich, growthy upper layer." There could be a corn crop and some potatoes the first year but two years were usually required to subdue the ground with plow, harrow, and cultivator. Because of marshy ground on part of his property, Store Per's first fields "clung to the contours of the uplands and hills."

Splitting rails and cutting posts was winter work in the Skunk River woods. From them Store Per made "worm" fences that twisted and turned to fit the irregular shape of his fields. When the soil was ready for grain Store Per sowed uniformly with a "measured tread, steady arm, and well calculating eye." Widened fields "gave evidence of gradual improvement," wrote Nehemias, the son of a pioneer, "and after some years crops flourished on the accumulated humus of centuries."

The Iowa Handbook for 1857 warned prairie settlers: "The immense mass of vegetation, dried by sun and frost, leaves the whole surface, except the cultivated fields, and water-courses with . . . combustible material. A single spark of fire, falling upon the prairie at such a time, instantly kindles a blaze that spreads on every side, and continues its destructive course as long as it finds fuel."

After describing an eerie nighttime fire several miles wide sweeping across the prairie, the author of the

Handbook, Nathan H. Parker, opined: "A narrow strip of bare ground, or a beaten road the width of a common wagon-track, will prevent the fire from spreading beyond it." Experienced pioneers knew better. According to Nehemias, they circled their homesteads with furrows about thirty feet apart and burned the grass between them. This hindered "advancing flames—sometimes the leader traveled at the rate of 30 miles an hour—from jumping over." Lazy farmers, Parker reported, allowed tall grass to connect their fields with the wild prairie, "and forfeit[ed] their year's toil as a penalty for their slothfulness!"

Fire was not the only threat to life and health. Pioneers and their doctors attributed a debilitating disease, malaria, to "bad air" arising from sloughs and marshes and from newly plowed prairie sod. Facts seemed to support this hypothesis because the incidence of ague, as it was also called, diminished with physical and chronological distance from the frontier. Store Per and others who had crossed the Mississippi knew that the disease was no longer the threat east of the river that it once was. They were confident that, in time, it would recede from Iowa too, and it did. Regardless of location, malaria sufferers experienced fevers alternating with chills. Even in midsummer they turned blue, shook, and their spleens enlarged. "Ague cake," they called this condition.

Store Per's determination likely matched that of his countryman Abram Holverson of Wisconsin, who, "attacked by a severe ague while breaking sod, simply stopped his oxen, 'lay down in the furrow to shake it out,' then 'gee-hawed' his animals and resumed plowing." Quinine alleviated the chills and fevers, but the settlers seldom summoned doctors or purchased expensive drugs. Malaria sapped energy which explains why some families progressed slowly, if at all.

All settlers needed potable water. Store Per believed that his flowing well would deliver an ample supply indefinitely. Most of the early settlers dug only ten to thirty feet for their drinking water. Shallow "slough wells" had a tendency to go dry in the middle of winter. One solution was to sink a well at the base of a hill and shore the shaft with masonry or planks. This took time and was dangerous work, but clean water then seeped in from higher elevations and provided a year-round supply to hoist to the surface with bucket and rope or hooked pole and pail. Prosperous pioneers succumbed to the salesmanship of "Pump Lars," the peddler whose wares reduced labor and made farm wives happy. As we shall see, dire consequences ensued when the flow of Store Per's artesian well slowed to a trickle in 1863.

Among the scores of people who, like Store Per, moved from the Fox River Settlement to southern Hamilton County were his brother Ole Andreas; their cousins Anders, Endre, and Christian Christenson; and the families of the Henryson twins, Torkel and Lars. Two of Store Per's sisters, Helga and Larsine, came directly from Norway along with their husbands. "Relatives and friends from Illinois as well as from the fatherland stream in great numbers to the new Norwegian settlement," reported Travaas.

People of other origins came too. In fact, the earliest settlers along the Skunk River tended to be rough-and-tumble Americans carried ever westward by the advancing frontier. According to Nehemias, "several so-called Hoosiers, typical rail-splitters, and a few Irishmen living along the river — stout, wiry fellows they were — . . . considered it a part of their creed to match strength amongst themselves or any from outside." The term "Hoosier" ordinarily applies to people from Indiana, but the Tjernagels sometimes used it generically to designate non-Norwegians who engaged in the process of pioneering. Among such people was "a big, muscular fellow" named Walter, the recognized champion. When Store Per arrived in the neighborhood "Walter eyed him with considerable interest and decided he would try to get the feel of him some day to determine what sort of stuff this big Norwegian was made of." Pugnacious Walter schemed for a bout but to no avail. Meanwhile, peaceful Per let it be known that "whatever of physical strength one possessed should be put to better uses than that of purposeless tussling," but if anyone attacked him he would have to defend himself. Learning this, Walter concluded that if there was to be action he must precipitate it. He would "watch his chance," then attack without warning.

> According to an eyewitness, the opportunity soon came. It occurred at a log-cabin bee where all the neighbors helped erect a house for an Irishman named Reagan. Walter and Per were there among the rest. Now or never, thought Walter; today shall decide who is the real champion in a trial of muscular might in this neck of the woods. As the call came for dinner and the men were leaving work, Walter suddenly leaped from the rear and set one of his knees in the small of Per's back, at the same time that he gripped him about the throat with a vise-like grasp to strangle him into submission. Per, however, though

surprised, took it calmly and deliberately reached a hand behind him, grabbed hold of the seat of his adversary's pants, and, catching him by the nape of the neck with the other, tore him loose and flung him several paces ahead of him, where he landed with a great smack on his stomach in the grass. The vanquished one rose without a word and made a beeline for home leaving his portion of the excellent meal untouched. Per walked on unperturbed, never as much as alluding to the short, but decisive, scrap.

While Store Per and the people who came with him to Hamilton County were establishing themselves as prairie farmers, an Illinois blacksmith, John Deere, was perfecting a self-scouring steel plow for breaking prairie sod. In 1860 he manufactured 1,200 of them at his company headquartered at Moline, but he could not keep up with demand. Deere's plow and a new federal land law accelerated settlement. To acquire title to a quarter section (160 acres), the Homestead Act of 1862 required only that a settler live on the land five years and improve it. Thus the Republican administration solidified its relationship with land-hungry Norwegian-Americans.

The Homestead Act, however, was of most benefit to those who settled west and north of central Iowa.

Chapter Eight

STORIES FROM THE PRAIRIE

Tell me the tales that to me were so dear,
Long, long ago; long, long ago.

The years Store Per spent on the Iowa prairie, 1857 to 1863, generated more stories about him than any other segment of his life. They tend to highlight his strength, sensitivity, restraint, helpfulness, good humor, and his ethnic background. In some instances readers may suspect that either Store Per or the storyteller is attempting to teach a lesson. For example, Peder Gustav presented a version of the Walter episode in *The Follinglo Dog Book*, which he wrote for his children. He might well have been instructing his sons in manliness, which, in Store Per's value system, did not include indiscriminate fighting.

The mature Store Per fought only when attacked, and then only defensively. In some instances Per used his strength to establish, in no uncertain terms, that Norwegians are not inferior to Yankees or other ethnic groups and must be treated with respect. Many of the stories that follow document change on the prairie.

In 1859, two years after Store Per settled in Iowa, his twenty-three-year-old brother, Ole Andreas, came from Illinois to pay a visit and buy land. With Ole was Malene's half brother, Christian Christenson. Both young men, natives of Norway, had been saving their earnings while "climbing the agricultural ladder" in the Fox River

Settlement with the intention of purchasing farms in Iowa. They rode the Rock Island Railroad to its western terminus at Iowa City, then walked the remaining 140 miles. As they neared their destination they stopped at the Hegland farm for a drink of water and were heartened to observe progress in the locality. Not only had the Heglands dug a well into a hillside but they had progressed beyond the bucket and rope method for raising water to a "chain-pump" system. After quenching their thirst and getting directions from Michael Hegland, they soon found Store Per in a small field "picking corn into a grain-sack."

Despite the crude realities of Store Per and Malene's "little log house," the "happy and contented" Hawkeyes showed their visiting siblings "noble pioneer hospitality." All shared what they knew about people and developments back in Tjernagel as well as about scattered relatives and friends in the United States including Jokum, Carl Magnus, and their families in Wisconsin; also about Peder Christenson, Aunt Kjersteen and their families in Illinois. Nobody knew what to make of troubling political developments in the United States, but Store Per and Ole Andreas were wary. Nevertheless, the cabin rang with music, laughter, and giggles from little Helga.

Store Per had a stack of unthreshed grain, "about as much as could be hauled in two loads, and a pig." The only thing that "lay heavily on his heart was the thought that if only these dear visitors had come a little later he would have had his grain threshed and the pig in the barrel, so he would have been able to entertain his guests in royal fashion." Store Per helped the land seekers find what they sought; both purchased land in the vicinity. Based on hard experience, Store Per saw to it that his brother's September 29, 1859, purchase of forty acres in section thirty of Norway Township from Isaiah Biggs for $180, along with ten-year rights to a timber tract, was duly recorded in Land Deed Book 2 page 443 in the new Hamilton County Courthouse in Webster City. Prosperity was returning and land prices were on the rise. The forty acres that Ole Andreas acquired became the core of Follinglo Farm and are owned by his descendants to this day. Their tasks accomplished, the two young men returned to Illinois.

It is not surprising that the visitors initially found Store Per in his cornfield. Maize fared well on newly broken ground. Settlers called it "sod corn." Store Per had also harvested some wheat, which would be threshed, taken to a mill, ground into flour, and consumed by the family as bread and other baked goods. In time, surplus wheat would become an important cash crop. In less than three years Store Per had built a log cabin, broken prairie sod, planted and cultivated crops, harvested them, accumulated livestock, built shelters for them, and he had also "put up considerable" hay.

The latter he cut with a scythe on the prairie, which also provided "free pasturage as well as winter roughage for his cattle." Back at Tjernagel North, Store Per's father, Lars, continued to dry hay on fence-like structures. This labor-intensive step in the haymaking process was necessary because of moist air on the seacoast and heavy dew at sixty degrees north latitude. In central Iowa, eighteen degrees south of Tjernagel and in the interior of a continent, farmers dried their hay on the ground.

Before stacking it they sometimes turned it with a fork or rake to hasten the drying process.

Following his visit to Iowa, Ole Andreas received the saddest letter of his life. His brother Store Per wrote that on October 24, 1859, a raging prairie fire overtook six-year-old Helga a quarter mile from her home and burned her to death. Ever after, when Ole Andreas related this tragedy to his children, it "always made us unutterably sad," wrote Nehemias. "Store Per . . . though powerful and quick of action in emergencies arrived on the scene too late to bring aid to his child."

A 1911 history of Hamilton County presented this commentary: "The one successful way" to fight a well-started prairie fire "was by starting a back fire." However, "backfires themselves sometimes proved to be nearly as dangerous as the original fires." In this instance "a neighbor woman" started a backfire "which the little girl and her mother," Helga and Malene, "had been helping to fight." The account closed matter-of-factly: "The little girl was burned to death." The thought of a mother seeing her daughter consumed in flames ignited by a neighbor intensifies the tragedy.

Into the twenty-first century descendants of Ole Andreas continue to tell their offspring about little Helga and how sensitive and loving Store Per was toward children after her tragic death. Malene had now given birth to three children but only one lived, Bertha Kjersteen, born May 29, 1859.

Natives of Norway generally feared snakes and conditioned their children accordingly. Several species inhabited the prairie. One day a girl named Julia who lived near Ole Andreas' farm told her father and brothers about an enormous snake she had spotted, but they laughed in disbelief. The next day Ole's boy Peder Gustav herded cattle with Julia. She again described the reptile, stressing its size. The curious children could not resist looking for it. Suddenly Julia screamed and clutched Peder's arm, which turned limp. She pointed to an enormous coil near a compass plant. "A snake like this I had never seen before," explained Peder as an adult, "nor have I ever seen one since. . . . [I]t was one rod long and in perfect health. The markings were the same as an ordinary bull snake or rattlesnake, but in place of dark gray spots it sported red spots." Stunned for a moment, the terrified children then fled as fast as they could run.

Almost as frightening to young herders were the unrestrained horses and wild bulls that periodically stampeded across the prairie as thunderously as Thor himself.

Acre by acre the open prairie gave way to the plow. This came none too soon for Store Per who witnessed only the beginning of the transition from prairie to "corn belt." Actually, two types of prairie made up the landscape in Story and Hamilton Counties, wet and dry. Detractors referred to Iowa as the "Frog State." The only jumping-off places for frogs, they said, were the knolls that rose above the sloughs and marshes. Large-scale drainage projects did not begin until after Store Per's time.

One day when cattle still roamed freely in southern Hamilton County a cow belonging to Store Per's neighbor ventured too far into a marsh and became hopelessly mired. The cow's owner and others worked long and hard to extricate her, "but the more they pushed and dragged the deeper she sank." When they were ready to give up, put the cow out of her misery, and salvage the meat, along came Store Per. He was not dressed to meet the demands of the occasion "because his footgear was a pair of wooden shoes of his own make, and they were not quite the thing for a quagmire."

The men told Per that the animal was doomed; "there was no use in wasting any more time and energy out there in that mud." Store Per responded that "he did not know if he could do anything," but he would try. "He shuffled through the reeds to the entrapped animal, selected the best possible footing, took good hold, and lifted the helpless creature clear of the mire." However, "the same power that brought that cow up forced him down, and we need not guess how the wooden shoes

fared. He did not even try to recover them. He said he could make a new pair easier than dig those out," and walked home in his stocking feet.

Store Per made himself useful in his community. The last glacier had deposited gravel in his neighborhood which enhanced his eligibility to serve as Norway Township's road supervisor. "When hauling dirt in his wagon during road work Per preferred to throw in his huge spade-fuls with one hand," testified an eyewitness, "enabling him to do quicker work, as well as to avoid bending his back."

Nehemias and Peder Gustav both penned versions of an episode in which Store Per's authority as road supervisor was challenged. In open defiance of the law and the public weal, a burly blacksmith named Knut Egland and his sons built a stout rail fence across the right-of-way of Norway Township's first road to keep roaming animals out of their property. Store Per asked the Eglands to remove the fence. He promised to take it down himself at a designated time if they did not comply. They taunted: "you can come, the fence won't move, but you will!"

At the appointed hour three "powerful specimens" of the Egland family found Store Per alone, nonchalantly "leaning up against the corner post." When he thought they had approached closely enough Store Per announced: "the show is on." With a burst of energy he "jerked up the corner post, and its appendaged rails" and warned: "my friends, you had better move, this fence will be coming your way!"

They moved.

Nehemias conceded that, in another sphere, the Eglands were true community benefactors. Knut developed an adaptive use for his blacksmithing tools; he pulled teeth for ten cents an extraction.

He would drop his horse-shoeing or other gainful work and expend much time and patience to relieve suffering. His wife, too, helped, steadying the patients while under operation and keeping their spirits up with encouraging words. On seeking the services of the formidable-looking pair — both were unusually large and strong — one felt as if in the grip of remorseless fate when held in position by Mrs. Egland's powerful arms, enabling Knut the better to manipulate the fearsome tongs. Some teeth seemed to defy removal, and then Maria's pity for the bleeding wretch in her arms would overcome her and she would cry out *"Naa drabe du an!"* (You are killing him!) But Knut thought it the greater mercy to oust the offending member at once, and wrenched and pulled till it surrendered its hold.

If Store Per went to the Eglands with a toothache he received his comeuppance for the fence episode.

How a settler used fences revealed much about his farm. If his main purpose was to fence roaming animals **out** of his farmstead he was still operating under frontier conditions. If, on the other hand, he fenced his cattle **in** so they could not roam and breed indiscriminately, the farm was more advanced. He was respecting his neighbor's property by keeping his cattle out of mischief and attempting to improve the bloodlines of his herd. Before the invention of effective barbwire in 1873 it was expensive and time consuming to build tight rail fences. But one could "read" a farm operation at a glance.

Years passed before Norway Township, Hamilton County, or any entity of government built bridges across the watercourses of central Iowa. The Skunk River did not rise as rapidly after heavy downpours as did the smaller streams and creeks, but one day when Store Per was away from home with Buck and Pride it rose precipitously. On his return trip he came to the familiar ford, saw danger, and lashed his wagon box to the truck. He then climbed on top of the load and, from his precarious perch, "gee-hawed" the oxen into the swollen stream. All went afloat but at mid-stream Pride submerged and came up under the wagon tongue in a deadly tangle with Buck.

Would this be the end of Buck and Pride, the span of oxen Store Per loved? Not if he could help it. "Not minutes, but seconds, would decide their fate." He dove into the river, under the tangle where the oxen frantically churned the water. He grabbed Pride by the horns and, quicker than can be told, released him from his yoke. The current carried Pride "blowing and snorting" downstream, but he was safe. This left Store Per and Buck with the wagon, battling the current which was gradually pulling the rig away from the landing place.

"Per now performed a long-remembered feat of strength and courage. He took Pride's place in the yoke and with united effort he and Buck managed to struggle ashore with the wagon and its contents." Meanwhile, Pride swam to shore and headed home. This left Store Per with no other alternative than to continue in the yoke, "and with Buck at his side he pulled his share of the load home three miles distant."

Until they produced significant quantities of wheat or livestock for the market, Store Per and his neighbors were subsistence farmers. The food that they raised for their own consumption differed in some ways from what they had known in Norway. Johnnycake (made of cornmeal), pork, beef, and wheat bread became dietary staples along with items with which they were familiar in Norway — milk products, potatoes, and garden vegetables. In Iowa they ate very little fish and much more

Beneath the surging waters of the Skunk River, Store Per releases Pride from the tangled traces.

red meat. Game inhabited the prairie and fish the Skunk River, but few pioneers found time for hunting or fishing. For the Tjernagels there was one exception; when someone took sick a determined family member went to the river for pike. Eaten fresh, it rested lightly on the stomach.

The standard grain in Iowa was wheat, as opposed to oats or rye in Norway. To be usable for home consumption, the wheat that Store Per planted, cradled, and threshed, also had to be milled into flour. Milling equipment required a greater investment than an individual farmer could make—a set of mill stones, a source of power, and a mechanism connecting the two. The man who became Iowa's Civil War governor, Samuel J. Kirkwood, operated a mill at Iowa City with the Iowa River as his power source. The earliest settlers of Story and Hamilton Counties transported their wheat by wagon to Kirkwood's mill until mills appeared closer to home.

The humorous side of Store Per surfaced when he "clubbed" with neighbors to haul wheat twenty-five miles to a new mill on the Boone River that advertised to the world that it operated day and night. Store Per and his neighbors planned to start grinding immediately upon arrival at the mill, bed down their draft animals for the night, and head home with their flour early the next morning. They arrived at the mill towards evening. "Imagine their disappointment, for no sooner had our settlers brought their sacks of wheat into the mill . . . before the machinery stopped and the miller shut down for the night."

This distressed Store Per and his friends because they carried sufficient provisions for their animals and themselves only for that night and the return trip the next day. Moreover, some of the wives back home "did not have enough flour from which to make a single cake or biscuit." The men "talked, begged, and implored" the grouchy miller to restart the mill, "but he turned a deaf ear to all their entreaty." Meanwhile, Store Per remained silent and in the background, but "looked as though he was revolving some plan in his mind."

> All of a sudden he walked over to his sacks, satisfying himself first that the miller took note of his actions, stooped down and took one sack between his teeth and one sack in each hand and walked coolly over to the hopper and set them down with a heavy thud, causing a slight quaver in the whole structure. He then started to untie the strings preparatory to pouring the contents into the hopper, when he was hailed by the miller who asked in no gentle manner what he was up to. Per answered him in his usual quiet manner, but he laid heavy stress on every syllable, "I am going to grind."

The miller started his machinery without delay.

The settlers needed sawed lumber for their larger and more sophisticated buildings. The following incident took place at Dan McCarthy's sawmill due east of Story City in the Skunk River woods. Lindsey Sowers, a participant in the action, related the tale to Store Per's nephew, Peder Gustav, who recorded it for his children in *The Follinglo Dog Book*.

> Mr. Sowers and three other Hoosiers came in, each of them with a load of logs. Per had come in ahead of them and stood waiting for someone that was ahead of him to get

unloaded. Of course he was next according to all rules, but the Hoosiers thought they would play him a trick and get into a fair and square fight with him. They reasoned like this: four strapping Hoosiers ought to be able to handle one Norwegian. They drove horses and had rather light loads on, while Per had his oxen [Buck and Pride]. They drove up and slipped past him before Per's oxen had even [as] much as pulled the slack out of the chain attached to the ponderous load behind them. They expected an immediate onslaught, but Per, instead of demanding his right as they had been looking for, let the Hoosiers have their own way and ordered his oxen to come to a halt. He stood there patiently waiting until they were through. Then he drove up to the place and commenced in the coolest kind of a manner to unload his terribly heavy logs. "But instead of putting them where we expected," says Mr. Sowers, "he rolled them right over our logs to where they really belonged. That took the fight out of us, because I doubt very much if all of us could have rolled one of those logs over those piles. Right then and there we made up our minds that a man who could control his temper like that and at the same time show us in the handling of those logs what he could have done to us, if he had been so inclined, was a man whose friendship it would be to our advantage to cultivate."

Although Store Per controlled his temper in this instance, he could not always do so. As previously related, while in port near Bergen as a young sailor he once lost his self-control, but diverted his aggression from a shipmate who had angered him to a tree which he battered with his bare fists.

He told his cousin Endre that a second episode that provoked him "nigh unto complete loss of self-control"

occurred when he became a Norway Township Trustee. Endre related to Nehemias that when Store Per assumed that position "he let it be clearly understood that all letters addressed to him were to be left unopened."

His wishes were respected until a letter came from Norway which a news-loving Norwegian neighbor, hoping to get fresh tidings from home, prevailed on someone in Per's family [likely Malene] to open. When Per learned of this he was sore displeased; and his irritation increased during the day, so much so that at chore-time in the evening he felt ire surging through his veins and vitals and finally into his throat, as he expressed it. Walking toward the dwelling at dusk he was conscious of relief at meeting no one, being uneasy about himself, for his passion had grown mightily upon him. Arrived before the threshold, his pent-up fury made him strike out at the hardwood logs by the door. Entering the house in a frenzy of spirit, it seemed as if a hand guided him to the

163

bookshelf and the Bible, wherein his eye fell upon the Book of Job, which he read throughout the night. Finally peace came to him and he asked forgiveness for his passion of God and those about him.

According to Endre, Store Per sometimes related this episode to admirers, "not wishing that anyone should think him perfect in self-control."

More typical of Store Per were the generous feelings he harbored toward his fellowmen, even when undeserving.

Having bought a patch of timber adjoining a much larger tract owned by another man, the latter, upon seeing the mass of driftwood which had lodged on Per's property during river-floods, though having enormous quantities of such wood on his own bottom lands, asked permission to help himself to Per's supply. Considering the circumstances, Per was much surprised at the unheard-of request, but, ever disliking to refuse a favor answered that he might take it if he needed it. Need or no need, the other took it, sure enough. Upon his wife's chiding him for such excessive large-heartedness, he said he felt sure they would have enough wood anyway, so why should he not please the other who took so much satisfaction in large accumulations.

A favorite tale of Store Per's nephews, Peder Gustav and Nehemias, stemmed from incidents in the 1860s when settlers were building substantial frame structures. Their versions differ in some details, but not in outcome. Peder reported that this example of his uncle's "great strength and cool mind" took place "at a barn raising at Lars Ostebo's place;" Nehemias that it took place at "Lars Henryson's place." There is no conflict here, this being an example of the confusion some Norwegians caused by using multiple names. Ostebo is the name of a farm south of Bergen near the village of Etne from whence he came. Therefore this man is Lars, twin brother of Torkel, sons of Henry from the Ostebo farm. Lars further confused the situation by sometimes using the name Henderson.

With allowance for Peder Gustav's exaggeration, this is what happened that day at Lars' farm.

All heavy dimension lumber in those days was hewn out of logs found in the timber. This was cut and mortised together where a barn was to be built, the framework was made ready into sections, and then a dozen or sixteen men were invited to the barn raising, and each section was raised and securely fastened. In this case, however, one of the sections was not secured sufficiently before the men let go of it. The natural result was that it started to come down. The people got panic stricken and started to scurry away from the terribly heavy section that it had taken sixteen men to raise; Per, however, had full control of his senses and the rest of his body as well, and knowing that if that thing was allowed to come down, someone would certainly get killed. He braced himself to meet it and held it all alone, and in his easy-going, well-calculated way of speaking said: "Don't get scared fellows, I've got it."

Nehemias regarded this as "the greatest lifting-effort of Per's life."

Store Per's construction skills went beyond cabin building, rough framing, and exterior carpentry. When a neighbor, Michael Hegland, built a substantial home he hired Store Per to do the plastering which "was done so well . . . that the material remained in place till lately," wrote Nehemias a half century later. "In calling to memory his friend Per," recorded Nehemias, "Michael remembered that he had had the honor of wrestling with

him and had been quickly thrown, though truth to say Michael was not so easily laid on his back in those days." In the same interview Michael expressed his affection for "his big, playful opponent and spoke with respect of this dear friend of his youth, known as the Strong Man of the prairies."

Hamilton County contained only 1,699 people in 1860. J. J. Wadsworth, a Yankee, ascended the hill to Store Per's cabin June 25 that year in the capacity of Assistant Marshal of the United States Census. He recorded the head of the household as Norwegian-born "Peter Larson," thirty-five, a farmer with real estate valued at $600 and a personal estate at $100. Had Store Per summed up his life that day, half way to an anticipated three-score years and ten, he would have concluded that it took him eight years in America to accumulate $700 in assets. But he was never one to measure success or failure in dollars alone. Back in Norway he had aspired to own his own farm. Now he owned one several times the size of his father's stony *gard*. A government soil survey once designated his township as "the best six miles square of agricultural territory in the United States."

According to the census taker, Per's Norwegian-born wife, age thirty-four, lagged behind her husband in formal learning. Wadsworth recorded her name as "Melinda," not Malene, and he checked the column next to her name headed "Persons over 20 years of age who cannot read and write." This is corroborated by legal documents she later marked with her X. There is no check beside Store Per's name. The enumerator recorded two other females in the household—daughter Bertha, age one, born in Iowa, and Ellen, Malene's half sister, thirteen, born in Norway. Thus Store Per and Malene gave a boost to a family member, just as Peder Christenson had done for them a few years earlier in Illinois.

Beyond the population schedule of the 1860 federal census, additional facts about Store Per's farm appear in Schedule 4, "Agricultural Products." The operation consisted of twenty "improved," and thirty-seven "unimproved" acres—large by Norwegian standards but small in comparison with his neighbors' farms. However, Store Per lagged in few categories of production and was particularly high in the production of potatoes (70 bushels) and hay (fifty tons). A table in the Appendix compares "Peter Larson's" farm with those of two peers in Norway Township, Lars Sheldall and Lars Henderson (Etne). None of these men owned oxen in 1860. Store Per had either worn out Buck and Pride or sold them to someone who intended to break sod.

Blessed with a loving wife, Store Per earned bread for his family by the sweat of his brow on his own land. He was happy working with plants and animals, especially during the warm months. Each autumn he offered a prayer of gratitude when persistent rains saturated the prairie tinder. Except for the loss of children, life was good for Store Per and Malene. The couple's fourth child, Lars Johan, born April 3, 1861, died December 17 that same year. The grief-stricken parents buried him next to his siblings in the family cemetery a short distance northwest of their log cabin. The strains of Store Per's violin could not dull the pain of losing Christen, Helga, and Lars.

Was this the price he and Malene had to pay for carving a farm out of the virgin prairie?

To persevere when winter set its icy seal on the land required character. On subzero days Store Per could do little more than feed and water his animals, fuel his stove, and contemplate nature's wisdom in protecting the topsoil with a blanket of snow. Fierce blizzards and drifting snow could quickly obliterate evidence of human presence on the prairie. "It happened, at times, that the little houses and sheds would disappear in the drifts at night, and in the morning a solitary chimney seen here

and there was about all the variety the landscape afforded." Snowbound Yankees were astonished when they first saw their Norwegian neighbors, children included, gliding about the countryside on wooden skis.

The restarting of nature's cycle made life worthwhile. Spring brought delicate shades of green, majestic wildflowers such as Queen of the Prairie, joyous songbirds, croaking frogs, sprouting blades of corn, and the incomparable aroma of native plumb and crab apple blossoms. "Bottled perfumes are unsatisfying by comparison," concluded Nehemias Tjernagel, a son of the prairie.

Chapter Nine
A SCHOOL, A WAR, SOME INDIANS, AND A CHURCH

A community is like a ship;
everyone ought to be prepared to take the helm.

Anticipation of sending Bertha off to school one day was motivation enough for Store Per to become involved in the founding of Norway Township's District School No. 1. The name "Peder Larson Tjernagel" appears in the list of the school's pioneer patrons. Built in the spring of 1860 by Lars Henderson (Etne), also known as Lars Henryson, out of locally milled lumber, the schoolhouse drew both Yankee and Norwegian-American children from southern Hamilton and northern Story Counties.

Adults enrolled too, including fresh arrivals from Norway who strove to learn the English language and American ways. Thus, seven-year-olds recited beside strapping farmers, among them Store Per's brother-in-law, Nils Peterson. Nils, who lived until 1913, liked to relate that the children "had a jubilee" when he first stood up to read out of McGuffey's *First Reader*. "But pretty soon," wrote Nehemias about his uncle, "the joke was on them, for after a few days when the advanced spelling class put on a performance, Nils . . . spelled down one of the star pupils."

Commonly known as The Sheldall School, after public-spirited Lars Sheldall who donated the building site, this useful institution adhered to high standards and helped transform Norwegians into Americans.

Regardless of ethnic background, pioneer mothers made their children's school clothes. "Kentucky-jean coats and pants, hickory shirts and heavy top boots for the boys were much in vogue. Calico dresses for girls had not gone out of fashion; and many pretty faces peeped out from beneath sun-bonnets those days." Thus, in outward appearance the children of Norwegian parents were indistinguishable from those of the Yankees—except in the dead of winter. Then the little Nordics came to school wearing warm stockings, mittens, and sweaters knit from wool in Old Country patterns.

The first teacher in the new schoolhouse, a Yankee, William A. Wier, hailed from New York. As a young man he had circumnavigated the globe as a whaler and then returned to the Empire State to become a schoolmaster.

He married and came west in 1856. An engaging man of diverse talents, he played several musical instruments and, like Store Per, had a fine singing voice. Into the twenty-first century his harpoon delights visitors to the original Sheldall School, which has been moved to Story City and restored.

Weir and his wife learned Norwegian so that they could interact with their neighbors, teach them English, and help them understand their adopted country. Hospitality to new arrivals was their hallmark. When tired parents and "tow-headed, grinning youngsters" stepped out of their prairie schooners at sundown the Wiers bedded them down for the night in their house. A son, Charles Francis Wier, remembered mornings with strangers "so thickly strewn around on the floor" that his mother had to step over them to make breakfast.

It is not difficult to imagine Store Per and William Wier swapping tales of the high seas, making music together, and enjoying each other's company at events in the Sheldall School, the center of community life in Norway Township. For reasons soon to be apparent, Wier taught only the 1860-61 winter term.

When Store Per and other freedom-loving Scandinavians contemplated coming to the United States they realized that an archaic institution, unknown in their culture since Viking days, cast a dark shadow over the southern part of the country. They read such writers as the Swedish traveler Fredrika Bremer who in 1850 labeled slavery "the great contested question of America, and will continue to be so, unless slavery ceases to exist there; because this institution is too evident a lie against the

American social principle, too crying an outrage against justice and humanity."

Among the people who came to the United States from Tjernagel in the 1850s, Jokum wasted little time to become a citizen, as previously related. Others, including Store Per and his brother, were more cautious. Although Ole Andreas took out his "citizen intent" papers in Illinois, he waited until the slavery issue was resolved "to renounce forever" his allegiance to the "King of Sweden & Norway" and become a citizen of the United States. He completed the process in the courthouse at Nevada, Iowa, April 21, 1868. Diligent searching has produced no evidence that Store Per took any measures to become a United States citizen.

It was difficult enough for the Norwegians to understand American government in the abstract. But while they were making farms, raising families, and creating institutions in the Midwest, forces drew these hyphenated Americans into a maelstrom. While contending for a seat in the United States Senate in the summer of 1858, a prairie lawyer and a railroad attorney who aspired to be president engaged in a series of seven debates that focused national issues for many Americans. The Lincoln-Douglas debates began at Ottawa, Illinois, a county seat town at the confluence of the Illinois and Fox Rivers in the Fox River Settlement.

There on August 21, Republican Abraham Lincoln and Democrat Stephen A. Douglas solicited support from a portion of the crowd that was just beginning to participate in politics. Both candidates affirmed the supremacy of the white race. But the tall man asserted that slavery was morally wrong and should not be extended. The "Little Giant" defended the Kansas-Nebraska Act of 1854 that he had authored. It repealed the Compromise of 1820 and opened Kansas and Nebraska to the possibility of slavery — territories previously closed to the South's "peculiar institution."

Would neighboring Iowa be the next state opened to slavery? Iowa's Republican governors answered with a resounding "No!"

Lincoln spoke of a court in Washington, D. C., that had decided that a black man named Dred Scott would remain a slave despite the fact that he had resided for years in areas closed to slavery. Lincoln did not approve the court's decision but could do nothing about it. More baffling to new Americans, voters could not cast ballots for either candidate in the 1858 contest. The state legislature in Springfield would decide who would represent Illinois in the United States Senate. The legislature returned Douglas, but Lincoln's reputation grew in the northern states and among the Norwegians. Store Per felt a special affinity to Lincoln; the two rail-splitters shared a February 12 birthday.

Because he had moved to Iowa in 1857, Store Per was not part of the crowd at Ottawa that opening day of the Lincoln-Douglas debates. However, residence on the Iowa frontier did not isolate him from the issues of the day. When the itinerant tinker and barber, Erik Magneson Kjyten, came to repair Malene's pans and cut Store Per's hair he brought partisan newspapers, some of them in the Norwegian language. Kjyten, "would tell interestingly of the political chaos in the South, of Indian disturbances in the Northwest, and of births, deaths, marriages and near marriages, and the general gossip in the older settlements from which his hosts had emigrated."

As he walked from cabin to cabin Kjyten carried a burning charcoal stove on his back "so placed in the pack as to obviate danger from fire." Consequently, a cloud of smoke preceded and followed his tutorials on national issues and how leaders in the Fox River Settlement, Koshkonong, and elsewhere were sorting them out.

Gradually, the Norwegians learned how American government worked, or was supposed to work. The main Norwegian language newspaper, *Emigranten*, launched in Wisconsin by the Rev. C. L. Clausen in 1852, initially favored the Democratic Party. That was two years before the founding of the Republican Party. There is no evidence that Store Per's offices of township road supervisor and township trustee involved partisanship, but trends were changing. South of the Hamilton County line in Story County a respected pastor, the Rev. Osmund Sheldahl, ran for the office of drainage commissioner on the Republican ticket in 1859 and won. Even local offices were becoming partisan.

By then *Emigranten's* editorial writers were advocating policies that resonated with Norwegian-Americans such as free government land and "no slavery for either blacks or whites." Subscribers increased. Historian Odd S. Lovoll has observed that *Emigranten* "worked for and was a part of" a swing on the part of the Norwegians toward the Republican Party.

When Lincoln ran against Douglas for the presidency in 1860, voter turnout tended to be light in the Norwegian settlements. Those who did vote overwhelmingly cast Republican ballots. According to Lars Johan Tjernagel, "only 13 or 14 votes" were cast in Norway Township, "with a big majority for Lincoln." (The walnut ballot box used in the election, a prime artifact in the Sheldall School for decades, has unfortunately disappeared.) Only one Democratic vote was cast in the township in 1860 and for many years thereafter. According to Lars Johan, "There was but one Democrat." Lincoln won the 1860 election with all of his electoral votes garnered in the North, which triggered secession. Rebel forces fired on Fort Sumter April 12, 1861; soon the United States was embroiled in a Civil War.

Discussion turned lively at the Sheldall School and throughout the land. When Iowa Governor Samuel J. Kirkwood called for troops to defend the Union, William A. Wier rallied to the call and the community lost the services of a valuable educator. He received a bounty of $100 for enrolling in Company K, Thirty-second Iowa Volunteers Infantry. The bounty, along with his army pay, went to support Mrs. Wier and their three young sons. Promoted to captain in the United States Army, Wier served until the end of the war. His example of service to the Union did not go unnoticed by his Norwegian friends.

Emigranten rallied support for the Union in another way. Its September 1861 issue carried Hans Christian Heg's stirring recruitment announcement: "Scandinavians! Let us understand the situation, our duty and our responsibility. Shall the future ask, where were the Scandinavians when the Fatherland was saved?"

Charles M. Johnson, who shared a wedding date with Store Per and crossed the Atlantic with him, is an example of a Swede who responded to Heg's call. He left a large family in the Wisconsin pinewoods and enlisted September 11, 1861. Severely wounded in the left shoulder during the siege of Vicksburg, he was discharged June 26, 1862. Charles lived out his life near the scene where he and the Tjernagel party were marooned in 1852. His injury entitled him to a lifetime pension of $2 a month.

Knut and Peder Phillops, unmarried sons of Kjersteen and Phillipus residing in the Fox River Settlement, responded to Heg's call by enlisting in Company F, Thirty-sixth Illinois Volunteer Infantry. The Phillops boys wrote home from the front in the Norwegian language; two of their letters are valued possessions of Knut's descendants. Peder, a particularly promising young man, died at Murfreesboro, Tennessee, December 1, 1863. After participating in seven major battles and suffering in Libby Prison and in a military hospital in Indianapolis, Knut mustered out October 4, 1864, and returned to the Fox River Settlement with an injured thigh. We shall encounter him again on familiar ground.

Another cousin of Store Per who enlisted was Christian Christenson, the young man who came to Iowa with Ole Andreas to buy land in 1859. He fell sick in camp, nearly died, and was discharged early in 1862. The war changed his identity. To honor a soldier he admired, he dropped the name Christenson and took the name Logan. After the war he farmed near Store Per's property where his descendants still live.

By one estimate, "one-sixth of the Norwegian immigrants let themselves be recruited whereas only one-eighth of all Americans signed up." In some units with high concentrations of Norwegians the carnage was staggering. The One Hundred and Fourth Illinois Infantry left La Salle County with 1,000 men and came back from a series of bloody battles including Chickamauga with 150. Although not of this unit, Colonel Hans Christian Heg of the Fifteenth Wisconsin Volunteer Infantry, the highest-ranking Norwegian to serve in the Civil War, died in the bloodbath at Chickamauga. His statue adorns the capitol grounds at Madison.

President Lincoln's proclamation of May 8, 1863, changed the status of "hyphenated" Americans with respect to their military obligations. Thereafter, "no plea of alienage" exempted from the draft "any person of foreign birth who shall have declared on oath his intention to become a citizen of the United States." Thus, Ole Andreas who had so declared in Illinois before moving to Iowa was subject to the draft; those Norwegian-Americans who did not take that measure were not.

The least likely man among Store Per's circle to show "real bravery on the battlefield" was his mild-mannered friend and neighbor *Taalige* Lars Henderson. Late in the war Lars "marched to the sea" as a private in Company I, Sixteenth Iowa Infantry. The timing of Lars' military service, as related to Store Per's life, is recounted in the next chapter.

With their men at the front it sometimes happened that women lived alone or with small children. Shortly after he came to Hamilton County from the Fox River Settlement in 1864, Nils Anderson Follinglo, great, great grandfather of this writer, heard someone cry out as he walked by a lonely farmstead. He entered the cabin "just in time to help usher a bouncing baby boy into the world." The mother was alone so Nils served as "nursemaid, cook and dishwasher till help could be obtained."

During his first summer in America Store Per had encountered Indians near Waupaca, Wisconsin. His skills and his violin playing helped keep the peace. The natives had already departed from the Fox River Settlement before he arrived there late in 1852. The situation was different in Iowa. Tribes that had once inhabited the central part of the state signed a treaty in which they agreed to move to Kansas by 1846. However, small bands that had lived among the Sac and Fox, Meskwaki they called themselves, trickled back to Iowa. During the same year that Store Per brought his family across the Mississippi, 1857, Iowa Governor James W. Grimes helped these peaceful bands purchase land on the Iowa River in Tama County. Their "settlement" was in the drainage basin just east of the Skunk River where Store Per lived.

Indian/white relations turned deadly in northwest Iowa early in 1857 when renegade Sioux avenged the killing of one of their own by a settler. Forty-two settlers died in the "Spirit Lake Massacre," a friend of Endre among them. One day in February "Two two-horse wagon loads of muskets" passed through Nevada "bound for Ft. Dodge." There was talk in Hamilton and Story Counties of converting some of the larger buildings such as mills into forts. "Some of the citizens of Story County left their homes and came to Nevada for protection and safety," wrote W. G. Allen in his history of the county, "but the scare was soon over, and they returned in peace to their respective homes."

Store Per brought his family to Hamilton County shortly after this crisis and simultaneously with the release of the last of the white captives. His encounters with Indians in the Hawkeye state were peaceful, approximating those of his relatives and neighbors. Endre told Nehemias that one Sunday (likely early in the Civil War) his mother looked out the cabin window during family devotions and saw what appeared to be a herd of cattle approaching. On closer scrutiny it turned out to be three columns of Indians, "with the central file heading straight for the house." Young men mounted on ponies "rode back and forth between the lines to communicate orders."

Frightened, Endre fled south with his family toward Store Per's farm. Along the way they met a neighbor who convinced them that there was no reason for alarm. So Endre paused and viewed an unforgettable "multi-colored pageant of the prairie winding in and out among the hills." A few "youthful stragglers brought up the rear and were crying." The settlers tried to learn the reason but to no avail. Peace prevailed. "The truth is," wrote historian Julian E. McFarland, "that at no time was any white person molested by an Indian in all of central Iowa!"

Spring and fall brought peaceful Meskwaki from the "Tama Settlement" to hunt, fish, and trap at their traditional campsites along the Skunk River. Settlers encountered them on the road to and from Marshalltown and at their woodlots near the river. Chance meetings sometimes resulted in trade. One Norwegian lad, Baara Erik, became the envy of his peers when his father came home with an Indian pony which Erik used for herding cattle on the prairie.

One day in 1864 when Ole Andreas was building a frame house on the land he had purchased in 1859, he was driving home from Marshalltown with a load of lumber. Several Meskwakis frightened him when they rode, single file, out of a grove in pursuit. Knowing that he could not outrun mounted horsemen with a lumber wagon, Ole proceeded at a normal gait. The Indians overtook and stopped him, then "formed a circle around the whole rigging, and commenced forthwith to clamor for tobacco." When convinced that he had none, they left.

On a spring day when Store Per's daughter Bertha and her cousin Peder Gustav were students at Sheldall School a band of Meskwaki camped less than a mile away on the Skunk River. The teacher, Lewis J. Anderson, saw an opportunity for his scholars to study "the real Indian." He asked if they would like to visit the camp. Hands went up and the students had an unforgettable day.

Peder Gustav recorded that they witnessed the young males "practicing with their bows and arrows, the squaws preparing the meals of soft shelled turtles, wood squirrels and other quadrupeds, the papooses rolling around on the ground, and an old warrior that had outlived his usefulness, covered with small-pox scars, leaning up against a tree smoking his pipe. Everything seemed to be accompanied by the musical Indian laugh," Peder Gustav reported, "except the old warrior who was just as sober as a sphinx, evidently nursing a grudge against his white brothers." The old man who remembered better days might have thought it ironic that the whites left their schoolhouse to learn about his people.

When Store Per first laid eyes on the virgin prairie of central Iowa he envisioned a peaceful community with one more dimension than Kleng Peerson envisioned for the Fox River Settlement. As recorded by Eric Arnesen

Travaas, Store Per thought how good it would be when he and his neighbors could some day call a pastor, build a church, and have it "just like it was" in Norway. During the 1850s when Norwegian Lutheran synods were forming and reforming in America, the organization closest to that standard was "The Synod for the Norwegian Evangelical Lutheran Church in America," commonly called the Norwegian Synod. Until such time when there would be a local Norwegian Synod congregation Store Per considered it his duty, as head of the household, to conduct family worship each Sunday. He was pleased to have left behind the religious discord of the Fox River Settlement.

During the month of June 1857, close to Store Per and Malene's arrival in Iowa, the Rev. Peter Andreas Rasmussen of Lisbon, Illinois, a faithful pastor well known to Store Per, delivered on his promise. He paid the first of his several visits to help the Norwegians near the Story/Hamilton County line found a church true to the spirit of the Lutheran reformation. "Every settler's home was visited by this zealous Christian man," wrote Ivar Havneros. "For the first time the precious Word of God was proclaimed in their new settlement." In anticipation of the day when a resident pastor could be called and a house of worship erected, "A kind of church order was established." From its very outset, "Peder L. Lien" was involved as member number thirty-seven of this tenuous congregation. Pastor Rasmussen returned that same fall and the settlers celebrated "real festival days . . . as long as the pastor was in their midst."

Store Per was then struggling with how he and his family would be known in their adopted country. The name

"Betsy Kristine," born "29 Mai 1859" to "Peder and Malinde Tjernagel" appears in a list of forty children Rasmussen baptized on visits prior to 1860. Some of these children were "old enough to walk up to the improvised baptismal font themselves." When Rasmussen came in 1860 he helped a committee, of which "Peder Larsen" was a member, draft a call letter to Nils Amlund (1830-1902), a fresh graduate of the University of Kristiania in Norway.

A "well bred bachelor," Amlund accepted the call, came to America, and was ordained in Chicago by the Rev. A. C. Preus. On the last leg of his journey in a lumber wagon, Amlund is reported to have exclaimed: "This must be the end of the world!" It did not take long for Store Per and a hundred settlers in Norway Township to think highly of Pastor Amlund. Like-minded regarding theology, they wanted an educated clergyman who would administer the Word and Sacraments in the manner of the Lutheran confessions and the State Church of Norway. They did not approve of emotional lay preachers who held noisy revivals, espoused a conditional gospel, judged others, and referred to themselves as "the" believers. The Rev. Amlund was the right man for them. As St. Paul wrote to the Christians at Rome: "How beautiful are the feet of those who bring good news!" (Romans 10:15) Pastor Amlund brought comfort to Store Per and Malene upon the death of their infant son Lars December 17, 1861.

In 1862 both Rasmussen and Amlund became Norwegian Synod clergymen. The congregation that called Amlund, The Norwegian Evangelical Lutheran St. Petri Congregation of the Unaltered Augsburg Confession, joined the Norwegian Synod that same year and also began construction of a sanctuary. St. Petri exists to this day in Story City but not in its original building. A busy man who traveled great distances to many preaching sites in homes, schools, and unfinished barns, Amlund nevertheless "dressed very properly as suited one of the cloth." It was a bonus for Store Per that his pastor "encouraged good music and song."

"Now Per had his wish fulfilled," concluded Travaas. "Now he, as well as all the other settlers, could go to church, . . . sing the same lovely old hymns as before, sit with attention, and listen to the blissful words that streamed from the young pastor's lips." To both paraphrase and quote St. Paul, Rasmussen planted the seed, Amlund watered it, "but God made it grow." (1 Corinthians 3:6)

Although Store Per likely helped during the early phases of construction of St. Petri's sanctuary, he never worshiped there. He died before the building was completed. More to the point, he and his neighbors ordinarily worshiped at what was known as St. Petri's "north circle" which met at Sheldall School. Nehemias Tjernagel, both baptized and confirmed by Amlund, stated that the beloved pioneer pastor seated his confirmands in a row "according to greater or lesser degree of dumbness." Without disclosing which one, modest Nehemias claimed to have "held up one of the ends." The students would have preferred "an endless chain." Lack of funds, the Civil War, and synodical strife explain why no church building arose in Norway Township until long after Store Per's time. Not until 1894 did North St. Petri Evangelical Lutheran Congregation raise its spire above the prairie. This writer's mother was baptized and confirmed there by Norwegian-born Pastor Gilbert O. Paulsrud.

In his history of Sheldall School Nehemias recorded that, in the pioneer years, "The school house being the only public building in the vicinity was frequently used for church purposes or other meetings of a public character. Rev. Nils Amlund, the resident, pioneer pastor of this section, often conducted divine services here. There were not a few baptisms; also marriages and funerals." One of the funerals was Store Per's and it came all too soon.

Before turning to that subject, let us view the big Norwegian of Norway Township through the eyes of two men who knew and admired him. Both views date from the Civil War. The first is from Charles Francis Wier, son of the schoolteacher, Civil War soldier, and first mayor of Story City. The setting was the western slope of what is now Story City's Fairview Park where several young men had gathered for an exercise of strength.

> Some large salt-barrels had been deposited there, and it was considered quite a test of strength to lift one of these into a wagon single-handed. A few of those present succeeded in performing the feat, but many failed. Along came Store Per bound for home; but he found his way blocked by lifting enthusiasts who begged him to join them in their pastime. He was finally induced to make the attempt, but lifted the barrel slowly into the wagon with a deprecatory air as if half ashamed of himself for taking part in such pranks. But as he happened to overhear considerable self-praise among those who had performed this 'next-to-impossible' feat he playfully took a barrel

under each arm, carried them a distance, laid them lightly on the wagon, and smilingly said: "I just wanted to let you see how some of us did it back in the ship wharves in the old country when we were a little rushed that was all."

The last tale to be related dates from late in Store Per's life. It appears near the end of Erik Arnesen Travaas' account of the central Iowa pioneers:

> Of course, Per had now gotten older but had not lost his strapping figure. He didn't waste his superior strength on unnecessary things, and therefore his many neighbors had great respect for him and regarded him as a really good-natured giant among them. When some arrogant Yankee acted smart, people just called on Per, and then the Yankee tramped away.

Occasionally, however, a feisty German, Yankee, "or whatever he was," challenged Store Per. Travaas recorded what happened one day when a challenger came to Per's farm and found him plowing:

> He didn't worry that he might get a beating. Calm, as he always was, he knelt down on one knee, put his left hand behind his back, and then with his big calm eyes fastened on the Yankee said, "In this position you may have permission to challenge me, and I shall never be worth being called a Norwegian if I can't, with one hand, throw you dead to the ground. Try now if you will."

Per likely intended the uncharacteristic threat as a deterrent to violence. It worked. "Frightened over Per's calm demeanor, the scoundrel ran as fast as he could."

The mature Store Per strove to pattern his life after a pertinent section in the Old Testament Book of Jeremiah (9:23-24): "This is what the Lord says: 'Let not the wise man boast of his wisdom or the strong man boast of his strength or the rich man boast of his riches, but let him who boasts boast about this: that he understands and knows me, that I am the Lord, who exercises kindness, justice and righteousness on earth, for in these I delight,' declares the Lord."

Store Per did not boast of his might, but he reigned as the strongman of his community until the day he died.

Chapter Ten

DEATH OF STORE PER

The old man has death before his eyes;
the young man behind his back.

The pivotal year of the American Civil War, 1863, opened with President Lincoln's Emancipation Proclamation. Store Per had no reason to suspect that death would soon overtake him or that his father would outlive him. But death came soon and unexpectedly to the thirty-seven-year-old from causes unrelated to the war.

This chapter and the Epilogue place Store Per's life in perspective and his death in context.

To summarize, the beginning of Per's life was recorded at Moster Church with a continuity going back to the origins of Christianity in Norway. He grew up in a culture steeped in tradition, surrounded by physical evidence of a deep past. Nature was against the people of Tjernagel. That made them hardy, concluded Lars Johan Tjernagel, Store Per's nephew. Were it not for the sea "they could not have existed." Not only did they depend upon the sea for food, many young men of Store Per's station in life had no other alternatives for employment in their native land than to become sailors or fishermen. Life in these occupations was hard and dangerous, with long absences from home and insufficient income to support wives and families. Eyes gazed westward across the Atlantic Ocean.

In 1852 Store Per married his cousin Malene and the couple sailed to the United States, brimming with plans for starting a family and acquiring a farm. With others from Hordaland, they proceeded to the agricultural frontier where the veneer of civilization was thin. They lived several months in Wisconsin and nearly five years in the Fox River Settlement west of Chicago where their first two children were born. In 1857 they left a religious "hornet's next" with eighty like-minded people, bound for central Iowa.

Here on the prairie Store Per and Malene fulfilled their dream of land ownership within sight of the tree-lined Skunk River in southern Hamilton County. They built a cabin on a gentle slope and subsisted on what they produced. They persevered through severe weather and economic depression. In the words of Lars Johan, they overcame "fever and ague and starvation." In a few seasons their efforts yielded crops and livestock to sell. Nevertheless, they paid a greater price for their farm than dollars could measure; a prairie fire took the life of their daughter Helga.

After he put down roots, Store Per seldom traveled any distance from home. A devout Christian and public-spirited man, he participated in the founding of a school and a church, built roads that intersected with Indian trails, and served as a township trustee The musical tradition in southeastern Hamilton County "began with Store Per," concluded musician and composer Nehemias Tjernagel. Indeed, the strains of Per's violin at Sheldall School signaled the arrival of culture in that locality. In an entirely different sphere, Store Per raised his neighbors' spirits with feats of strength, some of which served notice that Norwegians were ready to assume responsibilities in their adopted country.

Most people who came to the young republic from Northern Europe, Store Per included, were in tune with American democracy. However, by the late 1850s the course laid out by the founding fathers appeared to be blocked. The election of Abraham Lincoln to the Presidency in 1860 set off waves of secession that took eleven southern states out of the Union. Few questioned that preservation of a barbaric institution was the root cause of this disruption.

How would freedom-loving Norwegians with no prior experience with the institution of slavery and limited understanding of the American political process respond to this crisis? Whose leadership would they follow?

In 1901, the Rev. Ulrik Vilhelm Koren (1826-1910), Bergen native and long-time president of the Norwegian Synod, reviewed the momentous issues of 1860-61 that he had lived through. "Could war be avoided?" he asked the students at Luther College. "Could it be avoided other than by destroying the Union, ruining the Constitution and the work of the fathers, dissolving the United States and having a hostile power and government with slavery as its basis established right alongside?"

Koren and a high percentage of his countrymen were among those in the North who concluded that the Union must be preserved. Many of them had been favorably disposed toward the Republican Party and Abraham Lincoln since the Lincoln-Douglas debates. When war broke out young men in the Norwegian settlements answered Lincoln's call to arms. "I had held farewell services for those of our boys who went to war," wrote Koren about his ministry on Washington Prairie in northeast Iowa, "and regularly had greetings and letters from them while they were in the field or in the field hospital." The same must have been true for Pastor Amlund of Story City.

Early in the war things went badly for the Union. Iowans had particular reasons for apprehension. On August 10, 1861, confederate forces overwhelmed a Union army of 6,000 at Wilson Creek near Springfield, Missouri, the state just south of Iowa, and killed the commanding general and many soldiers from Iowa.

As months wore on and casualties mounted, it became increasingly clear that this would be a war against the institution of slavery. The Emancipation Proclamation clinched the matter. According to President Koren, Norwegian Synod clergymen "were all anti-slavery men." That generalization included the pastors who served Store Per—A. C. Preus temporarily at Koshkonong, Rasmussen in the Fox River Settlement, and Amlund in Iowa. Nevertheless, abolitionists derided Norwegian Synod people as defenders of slavery because they would not deny that some New Testament Christians owned slaves and that "the apostles did not demand that they should be freed, but that they should treat them as brethren." Holding to the accuracy of Scripture was more important to Synod leaders than pleasing abolitionists. As new Americans, they did not possess the acumen to phrase their positions in words acceptable to groups with whom they essentially agreed.

Store Per did not fight in the Civil War nor did his brother Ole Andreas. Men close to them did fight, some of whom made the supreme sacrifice. They understood and supported President Lincoln's goals of preserving the Union and abolishing slavery. By and large, the population of Iowa did too. Mortality of Iowa soldiers from all causes as a percentage of white males ages eighteen to forty-five residing in the state in 1860 was 9.3 percent — second only to Indiana's ten percent.

North of the Iowa border in the Minnesota River Valley, conflict of a different type broke out in 1862. Late government payments to the Dakota Sioux, land cessions, and crop failures touched off hostilities that resulted in cabins burned and hundreds of settlers slain. An army consisting mostly of militia defeated the Sioux, thirty-eight of whom were hanged at Mankato December 26, 1862. Had President Lincoln not intervened, 303 would have been executed.

Just as he had protected women and children a decade earlier in the Wisconsin wilderness, Store Per reasoned that, for now, his place was at home with his daughter Bertha and his wife Malene who was due to have her fifth child in February 1863.

Discussions certainly took place between Store Per and his friend and neighbor, *Taalige* Lars Henderson, about national issues and military service. It is possible that they planned to enlist together at an opportune time, just as they had collaborated in other important decisions affecting their lives. Late in the war *Taalige* Lars did enlist, under circumstances to be related shortly.

Store Per did not live to see the tide of war change at Gettysburg and Vicksburg in July 1863, much less to witness an end to the institution of slavery and the return of peace to his adopted country. Norwegian Synod President Koren could not imagine a leader equal to the challenges of those times "arising anywhere else than from the circle in which God had him arise, among new settlers in America's western states." He shared that insight in his "Lincoln's Birthday" lecture at Luther College in 1901, published his remarks, and the assessment resonated with Norwegian-Americans.

The most credible account of Store Per's death comes from his niece, Bertha Kjerstine Tjernagel, sister of Lars Johan, Peder Gustav, Nehemias, and Helge Mathias. A trained nurse, she cared for Endre Christenson during his waning days in 1922. Not only had Endre been Store Per's companion during their years as sailors and during the Atlantic crossing, the two were together that fateful last day of February 1863. Ten days earlier Malene had given birth to her fifth child, another Peder Larson Tjernagel. Endre related the following details to Bertha which are supplemented with additional facts that he communicated to her brothers on other occasions.

Endre believed it relevant that Store Per's well had gone dry that February—an inconvenience both to his household (including newborn Peder) and to his livestock operation. The predicament was all the more vexing because of the time of year and because the family had come to rely upon their artesian well. Lars Johan explained in a 1938 newspaper article that sand and grit sometimes slow flowing wells to a trickle. His own artesian well in Story City had been discharging water since 1889 at the rate of ten gallons per minute. During those forty-nine years he calculated that it had "ejected 257 million gallons of water." A retired lawyer, Lars Johan ordered his well "vacuum cleaned" whereupon it resumed flowing.

Store Per did not have that option. Despite the fact that it was February, he rolled up his trousers and began digging. "When he struck a spring he stood there in the cold water working. . . . Endre believed standing in that cold water bro't on the Colic."

Nevertheless, Store Per made preparations to go to Marshalltown to trade February 27, 1863, a Friday. He no longer owned Buck and Pride but now used a team of fast horses for such trips. The fact that he planned to sell a dressed hog so that he could "buy something for his remaining girl and his wife" is evidence that the farm was producing a surplus. Sociable Per disliked traveling alone so he asked Endre to go with him. Endre had made prior arrangements to take a load of grain to a mill on the Iowa River near Marshalltown. So the cousins agreed to meet at Zearing and make much of the trip together.

Endre arrived at the meeting place but Store Per did not show up. Endre "became anxious," went to look for his cousin, and learned from a traveler that Store Per "had gotten so sick on the prairie he couldn't drive his horses." Peder Gustav adds: "He came as far as about where the town of Zearing now is situated, when he was suddenly stricken with a severe pain in his abdomen. His otherwise powerful hands let go of the reins, and his spirited horses started to run." Others caught the team and carried stricken Per to a farmhouse. When Endre arrived Store Per lay "praying to be allowed to go home." In dire straits, he could not be moved. People scurried to summon a doctor and close relatives. "Endre stayed with him '*ti de of daga*' (daybreak)." Store Per told the people of the house "that God would pay them for their kindness to him."

A doctor came but his license had been revoked "and he didn't dare do anything." Before loved ones arrived, Store Per died early in the morning of Saturday February 28. Endre concluded that a "membrane '*ne for bringo*' (below the chest) broke." Perhaps an abdominal aortic aneurysm had burst.

And so it was that relatives and neighbors came to the Sheldall School for Store Per's funeral. No account of it survives, but it is not difficult to imagine what transpired. Men and women gathered that early March day in their blue twill, and children in the best clothes their mothers had made for them, to pay respect to a man they loved. "Their looks were in truth not very charming," wrote a contemporary about these very people. "They didn't think they were better than they were, namely poor settlers."

198

Pastor Amlund was then in Norway to fetch his bride. Therefore, a pioneer pastor of Story County, the Rev. Osmund Sheldahl filled in for him, brought comfort to the bereaved, reminded all that a redeemed sinner was in his heavenly home, and summarized Store Per's life of thirty-seven years. Norwegian Synod congregations commonly sang *"Den store hvide Flok vi se"* at funerals. Based on the seventh chapter of *Revelation*, here is the first verse, translated into English:

> Behold a host, arrayed in white,
> Like thousand snow-clad mountains bright;
> With palms they stand. Who is this band
> Before the throne of light?
> Lo, these are they, of glorious fame,
> Who from the great affliction came
> And in the flood of Jesus' blood
> Are cleansed from guilt and blame.
> Now gathered in the holy place,
> Their voices they in worship raise;
> Their anthems swell where God doth dwell
> Mid angels' songs of praise.

The strings of Store Per's violin knew well the haunting Norwegian folk melody that gave loft to these words. The instrument that had stirred hearts on two continents and on an ocean between them remained silent that day. When Per's father back at Tjernagel North received a letter informing him of his son's death he remarked, "I do not need any more letters from America." Lars Johanneson lived another fifty-three days and died April 22 at age sixty-nine.

Store Per, Peder Larson Tjernagel (1826-1863), lies buried near his prairie home in Boe Cemetery on a picturesque horseshoe bend of the Skunk River. Beside herself from grief, Malene "had to be watched for a week" following her husband's death. Bertha Tjernagel learned from Endre that she "Wanted to tear her clothes off." Yet another cruel blow fell August 15, 1863, when her son, Store Per's six-month-old namesake, died. He is buried beside his father. Now, Malene's husband and four of her five children were in untimely graves.

Anna and *Taalige* Lars Henderson were among those who extended help during those trying times. Then, on July 3, 1864, Store Per's youngest sister, Larsine, arrived from Norway with her husband Nils Peterson. For a time, Nils work-ed the farm. It was not until af-ter he and Larsine were on the scene that *Taalige* Lars joined Sherman's army and did his part to bring the war to a close. Back home after the war Lars re-sumed his char-acteristic kindli-ness and mod-esty. He attended meetings of the Grand Army of the Republic until he died in 1908.

Taalige *Lars Henderson in later life as he went off to meetings of the GAR*

One way to sum up a man's life, not the most revealing in Store Per's case, is to examine his estate. Store Per died intestate. Under Iowa law, both his widow and his minor children had rights. By the time legal wheels began to turn, Bertha was Store Per and Malene's only living child. The "State of Iowa, Story County" appointed a guardian for her and ordered an appraisal of "all the personal property and Real Estate of Peter Larson," which the court received July 19, 1865. The guardian had the authority to "set off and allow to the widow, and children under the age of fifteen years" provisions for their support. Household goods, the cabin, outbuildings, and the land upon which they stood were part of Malene's dower, which consisted of one third of the value of the estate. The rest went to Bertha.

Real Estate 53 Acres at ten Dollars per Acre	530.00
Temer Land 5 ½ Acres at ten Dollars per Acre	51.00
Money an Intrest	520.00
Neat Cattel	60.00
Plow	10.00
	$1171.00

Lars Henryson prepared and signed the appraisal in his capacity as Justice of the Peace. It is apparent that he had not yet mastered the English language.

The fifty-three acres constitute the farm, most of which was above the surrounding wet prairie. The land had increased in value from $3 per acre when Store Per bought it from Alpha Person in 1858 to $10 per acre in 1865. The "Temer Land" was Per's timber lot on the Skunk River. The "Money an intrest" likely came from the sale of woodlots or other real estate Store Per had once owned. "Neat" cattle, according to a dictionary of the period, were "all kinds of beeves, as ox, cow, steer or heifer." The face of the inventory shows the first name of the deceased in the English and American manner, "Peter." The verso of the same document has it "Peder" — unwitting evidence of his split national loyalties. Had he lived to three-score years and ten and followed the pattern of his brother he would have become more thoroughly American and he would have standardized his name.

To tie up the strings of our story, Malene (1827-1896) continued to live on the farm with her daughter Bertha. Variations of her name appear in court records, but she consistently signed legal documents with an X. When combat-seasoned Civil War soldier Knut Phillops came home, wounded, to the Fox River Settlement in 1864 he was "very much grieved" upon hearing of the death of Store Per. A man of "quick decision," Knut remarked to his parents, Kjersteen and Phillipus, "we go to Iowa as quick as we can get there."

They did. Knut, nine years younger than Malene, took a turn at working the farm. After he settled his parents and nieces, Dorothy and Julia, on an acreage near Story City, he married his cousin Malene July 9, 1865. In coming years Knut expanded the operation from Store Per's "partly improved" acres to an entrepreneurial farm of 400 acres with substantial buildings, including a large barn with an artesian water system that was a model in its day. Two children were born to them. Petra died in infancy. The second, Peder Martin, added forty acres to "Fairview Farm" and lived a long life there. In 1900 he operated a "22-position farm," meaning that a labor force of that number was required at grain threshing time.

Bertha Kjersteen Larson (1859-1932), Malene and Store Per's only child to reach adulthood, was treated well by her guardian. After she came of age the Circuit Court discharged him from his duties. Two weeks later she married the hired man, Samuel Espe, March 8, 1878. Before the year was out she bore the first of her ten children. As she matured she developed a big heart for Christian missions. Like her father, she was exceptionally strong. "It was said of her that when she was in her prime, and her husband brought home a barrel of salt, she would lift it out of the wagon, and carry it down into their cellar." A standard barrel of salt weighs 280 pounds.

In the 1970s Bertha's daughter Clara Malinda Espe became the subject of an oral history interview. She related that when she was a girl her grandmother, Malene, told stories about her first husband's feats of strength, especially the one about pushing covered wagons out of the mud en route from Illinois to Iowa. Clara made certain that the interviewer understood that her grandfather was known as "Store Peer, Norwegian for very big, next to a giant."

What became of Peder Pederson, Store Per's son by Johanne back in Norway? His mother and stepfather, Mathias Jacobson Kallevik, raised him as a farm worker and witnessed his confirmation September 8, 1861. Helga Kallevik, a descendant of Johanne and Mathias who lives on the historic Kallevik farm at Mosterhamn in Bomlo commune, has sifted sources and has found a few facts about the remainder of Peder's life.

At age nineteen he left home and moved to the Melkevig farm on the island of Stord, due north of Tjernagel. He died there at age twenty-one August 11, 1866. He never married and he had no children. Thus there are no descendants of Store Per in Norway. Peder Pederson is buried in Finnas Parish where he grew up.

Kjersteen Phillops, Knut's mother and Store Per's Godmother, brings our story full circle. She had been midwife (*hjelpekone*) at the birth of Store Per February 12, 1826, at the birth of Ole Andreas April 10, 1836, at the birth of Peder Pederson March 12, 1846, and, in the course of her ninety-one years she delivered numerous children in Norway, at Koshkonong, in the Fox River Settlement, and in Iowa. As Peder Gustav explained, this hardy woman had "faced storms and blizzards without any thought of ever being compensated." Her main worry was, "will I get there in time to be of any real service?"

On *Syttende Mai* 1865, Kjersteen arrived at Follinglo Farm in section thirty of Norway Township in time to attend the birth of Martha Karina and Ole Andreas' second child. After the mother delivered, the seasoned midwife announced excitedly in the Norwegian language: "It's another Big Peter, and weighs thirteen pounds, and you must call him Peter!" The parents acquiesced.

History so unfolded that the present writer was the first male child born in Peder Gustav Tjernagel's direct line following his death in 1932. That is why I received the name Peter Tjernagel Harstad. Not from books, but from two generations of Tjernagels before me, I first heard the Store Per stories.

When Nehemias summarized Store Per's life he reported that eyewitness informants agreed "that this man possessed great muscular strength, that he had a fine disposition and a staunch character, and that he was loth to display his exceptional physical powers unless the exigency of the occasion demanded it."

With vestiges of Norwegian accents in their voices and vocabularies suitable for my years, this is the essence of what Nehemias, Lars Johan, and their sister Bertha told me about their uncle as I was growing up.

From p. 1 of Nehemias Tjernagel's scrapbook in the Tjernagel Collection at the State Historical Society of Iowa in Iowa City. Nehemias' caption reads: "Peder Larson-Tjernagel, born Feb. 12, 1826, died Feb. 28, 1863. 'Store Per.' Married Malena Christianson. Children died young, except Bertha." Other photographs of Malena exist, but this is the only known photograph of Store Per.

EPILOGUE

Peder Larson Tjernagel (1826-1863) and Henry David Thoreau (1817-1862) were contemporaries but they viewed the American frontier from vastly different perspectives. Himself a frontiersman, Store Per labored to make a farm for his family out of virgin prairie in Hamilton County, Iowa.

Surrounded by his books in Massachusetts, Thoreau viewed the frontier from afar, not as a physical place but as a metaphor. For him, the frontier was not "east, or west, north or south; but wherever a man fronts a fact." Let that man "build himself a log house with the bark on where he is, fronting IT," and wage war with "whatever . . . may come between him and the reality, and save his scalp if he can."

For centuries people have come to America to make something of themselves and the opportunities they perceive. They came from all parts of the globe and developed mindsets that have become part of the American character. It is now a "given" that one must not remain idle where there is opportunity. The western frontier is long gone, but Americans need to be reminded that millions continue to look to the United States for opportunity. State Department officers in foreign lands report that every business day people line up to seek American citizenship. A journalist born in India who himself became a citizen, wrote in *Newsweek* (June 11, 2007, p. 28): "every year we take in more immigrants than the rest of the world put together." Fareed Zakaria argues that this enriches the United States and gives it advantages in a highly competitive world of global perspectives and markets.

Confronting difficulties, head on, as advocated by Thoreau and practiced by Store Per, is another component of the American character. In Per's case the same lush prairie vegetation that nourished his livestock brought devastation, including the death of his daughter.

The issue became: How does a man respond when opportunity comes bundled with potentially lethal elements? Store Per had options. He could have left the agricultural frontier and gone back to the more settled parts of Illinois or even to Norway. Some did, and their peers did not think the less of them.

Many considerations go into the determination of character. While engaged in the ever-unfolding challenges of life, how does a man relate to his parents, his family, the opposite sex, his neighbors, the broader community, people of other cultures and races, and to his maker? How does he react when his country is in the throes of economic depression or at war?

Readers now know how Store Per acted and reacted in real-life situations. There is context for contemplating the measured ways in which he deployed his physical strength, used his sense of humor, and spent his allotted time.

Store Per and Thoreau looked at the world differently, but would agree that the great American metaphor, the product of generations of pioneering, must not be reduced to a formula for confronting challenges with positive attitudes and making the most of opportunities.

There must be room for spiritual dimensions and times and places for enjoying beauty in whatever form it may take.

This realization brought Thoreau to a mysticism of his own making.

Store Per took a different course. At the end of the day he took out his Bible and studied it with his family. When he turned to the Apostle Paul's letter to the Philippians 4:12 he took this admonition to heart: "work out your salvation with fear and trembling, for it is God who works in you to will and to act according to his good purpose." Per knew that, on his own, he could never be perfect, but always "in the making" by the power of God.

After family devotion he took out his violin and played melodies that reminded him of the fjords of western Norway.

Never fully Americanized, Store Per climbed the agricultural ladder to the rung of land ownership and farmed some of the best land on earth. Given his magnanimity, he would have nodded assent to an admonition that a son of pioneer parents, A. M. Henderson, delivered at an Old Settler's Picnic at Bell's Mill, Hamilton County, Iowa, Sunday, August 1, 1937: "Friends, let us American citizens never kick down the ladder by which we climbed up."

Given the venue at the mill, the realities of the Great Depression, and the fact that he sprang from people who "came here with the Word of God not only in their trunks but also in their hearts," Henderson went a step further and closed with this poem:

Back of the loaf is the snowy flour, and
Back of the flour the mill, and
Back of the mill is the wheat, and
the shower, and
the sun, and
the Father's will.

Store Per knew his Father's will. Spiritually, that meant that he relied solely upon the redemptive work of Christ to save him from sin and eternal death. Out of gratitude, he would strive to do good in an imperfect world.

In a secular or civic sense, was he a heroic figure? He did not consider himself such. If others would answer yes, is every man who overcomes difficulties, loves his wife, supports his family, and works for the good of his community a hero too?

A question lingers: How big was Store Per? We shall never know precisely because no measurements have come down to us. Only one photograph of him is known to exist. He looks powerful but the photograph shows only his head and shoulders.

His daughter Bertha was large and strong. On a family photograph she appears to be taller and broader than her husband, Samuel Espe.

Their son, Austin Espe, grandson of Store Per and Malene, stood just short of six feet tall but tipped the scale at 300 pounds. His son Leon states that Austin was solid muscle and patterned after Store Per. He had a large head, barrel chest, and thick forearms. Austin once submitted these measurements when ordering clothing out of a Big and Tall catalog: 22-inch neck, 52-inch chest, and 48-inch waist. Leon is taller than his father but not as heavy. Now in the prime of life, Leon's two solidly built sons stand taller—six feet five inches and six feet seven inches, respectively.

If such genetic evidence is pertinent, Store Per must indeed have been large.

APPENDIX

1860 Census, Schedule 4, Agricultural Product

Products	Lars Sheldall	Lars Henderson aka Henryson	Peter Larson (Tjernagel)
Improved acres	100	40	20
Unimproved acres	20	120	37
Cash value of farm	$1,000	$1,600	$600
Value of farm implements and machinery	$75	$80	$50
Horses	3	4	3
Milk cows	6	6	3
Working oxen	0	0	0
Other cattle	2	3	4
Sheep	0	7	0
Swine	3	4	4
Value of livestock	$350	$550	$400
Wheat, bushels of	40	73	20
Rye, bushels of	0	0	0
Indian corn, bushels of	200	50	100
Oats, bushels of	6	24	0
Wool, lbs. of	0	6	0
Irish potatoes, bushels of	25	10	70
Butter, lbs. of	500	500	300
Hay, tons of	20	25	50
Molasses, gallons of	4	0	0
Value of amounts slaughtered	$50	$25	$50

Information extracted by Arlen Twedt and used here with his permission.

THE AMERICA STONE

During an 1892 visit to Norway, Iowa-born Nehemias Tjernagel climbed to the crest of a ridge above the Tjernagel farms. "On one of its slopes," he wrote home July 18, "is a natural stone hut . . . called Anders *huse*, where father and many others had rested when herding sheep in ye olden days. I carved my name there."

Ninety-one years later, Norwegian relative Ole Andreas Olson Tjernagel led the author and daughter Karen through a peat bog and up the slope to the same site where we chiseled our initials into the rock July 5, 1983. Ole explained that only people of Tjernagel blood may carve their names here. We qualified, but my father, our translator, did not.

July 20, 2010, Helga Reinertsen of the Tjernagel North farm led a party (including the author, my wife, daughter Linda, and her husband) to what is now known as "The America Stone." The photo on the left shows Linda viewing her father's and sister's initials and dozens of other names, some of them difficult to read.

The photo on the right shows historian Willy Mjanes (whose family has long owned portions of the nearby Lien farm) explaining to the author (with hat) a current belief that, prior to departing for America, emigrants carved their names here. In Norway, alternate interpretations often exist, side-by-side, to explain the same historical site.

ACKNOWLEDGEMENTS,
SOURCES, AND NOTES

Work on this biography began in June 2005, at the Gift of Life Transplant House in Rochester, MN, while the author (PTH) was undergoing a stem cell transplant at the Mayo Clinic. During the next five years the project brought me to people and sources in far-off places, often via the internet. This book and a documentary film produced and directed by my nephew, Nathan Harstad, and narrated by my brother, Mark O. Harstad, are the results.

The following people have provided sources, insights, or assistance: Melvina Aaberg, Norma Bakros, Linda Becker, Kari Bergeson, Dale Berven, Tova Brandt, Catherine Bue, Clarence A. Chicks, Elsie Christianson, Mark DeGarmeaux, Leon Espe, Kolbein Espeset, Elizabeth Fremming, Laurann Gilbertson, Terje Gudbrandson, Hans Gungsto, Sigrid Hanson, Carolyn Harstad, Herman and Cheryl Harstad, Grace J. Harstad, Nathan Harstad, Mark O. Harstad, David Henderson, Julie A. Hintz, Helga Kallevik, Lori Kloberdanz, Jennifer Kovorick, Kenneth Lederer, Susan Lederer, Odd S. Lovoll, David McDermott, Amanda and Norman Madson, Paul G. Madson, Fred and Margaret Matzke, Mark E. Maggio, Willy Mjanes, Dorien Myhre, Kathryn and Richard Munsen, Tim Neuroth, Roger L. Nichols, Mildrid Nickson, Torjus Nordboe, James P. Olsen, Philip T. Rhodes, Helga Reinertsen, Bernard and Ingeborg Schey, Karen Scislow, Steve Sheldahl, David Shold, Kolleen Taylor-Berven, Erling Teigen, Norman Teigen, Bertha Tjernagel, Gerald Tjernagel, John Tjernagel, Arlen Twedt, Susan L. Vande Kamp, Cheryl Weber, Marilyn Webster, and Richard Williams. Also Don Hill, Mary Moldstad, Greta Olso, and Ardis Petersen, now deceased. Details of how most of the listed people have helped appear in notes, but some did so in ways not directly related to a specific portion of text. Warm thanks to all.

During the gestation of this book I have communicated frequently with three people. Mildrid Nickson's knowledge of the Tjernagel family is encyclopedic. She supplied facts, answered questions, and corrected errors. Like the author, she descends from the Larson line of Tjernagels. Philip T. Rhodes (hereafter PTR), a "Christenson" Tjernagel, is the undisputed master of pertinent digitized sources on both sides of the Atlantic and an indefatigable scanner of documents and images. Phil's promptness and precision in responding to queries is phenomenal. Arlen Twedt, the driving force behind the Central Iowa Norwegian Project, has gathered a wealth of sources at http://genloc.com/NorStory/. He referred me to essential sources and searched his voluminous files to answer my questions. I am deeply indebted to Mildrid, Phil, and Arlen.

This story is spliced together from bits and pieces. Basic facts are grounded in sources identified in the text or in notes for the ten chapters. Collateral sources provide context. Much of this material came from four of Store Per's nephews, all sons of Ole Andreas Larson Tjernagel and his wife Martha Karina: Lars Johan Tjernagel (1862-1950); my maternal grandfather Peder Gustav Tjernagel (1865-1932); Nehemias Tjernagel (1868-1958); and Helge Mathias Tjernagel (1871-1940). Hereafter in the notes I refer to them by their initials.

NT's writings proved to be particularly useful, especially: *Walking Trips in Norway* (Columbus, OH, 1917), 269 pages; *Contributions to Church Periodicals* (Story City, 1955), 168 pages; Letters From Europe, unpublished, 1892-95, 234 pages; Letters From Norway, unpublished, 1910; The Passing of the Prairie, a large unpublished work housed in the State Historical Society of Iowa in Iowa City along with other Tjernagel material. Part one, organized topically with pages numbered 1-297, is cited below as Passing of the Prairie and a page number. Similar material appeared in eight articles in *Annals of Iowa* 1951-1954. Part two, not paginated consecutively, is now in print as *The Passing of the Prairie by a Fossil: Biographical Sketches of Central Iowa Pioneers and Civil War Veterans, Edited by Margaret Harstad Matzke With an introduction by Peter Tjernagel Harstad* (AuthorHouse, Bloomington, IN, 2009), 248 pages. A bibliography of NT's writings and musical compositions appears in pp. 81-84 of *Nehemias Tjernagel's Music: An Album* (Jackpine Press, Lakeville, MN, 2006) edited by PTH. During visits to Follinglo Farm in my youth NT's narratives enthralled me. Portions of this book are based upon what I absorbed from him, LJT, their sister Bertha, my mother, and relatives of her generation.

A few words about editorial policy. Whether Nynorsk or Bokmal, the Norwegian language, uses both diacritical markings and letters not ordinarily familiar to English readers. When presenting Norwegian phrases and proper nouns in some of his writings, NT omitted diacritical markings and substituted English letters for distinctive Norwegian ones. This policy has governed the preparation of this book. Great variation exists in the form and spelling of names in Norwegian and American sources. Except in direct quotations, the convention here is to standardize names in the form people settled upon in maturity.

Karyn E. Lukasek's role in the making of this book (described on the title page) is gratefully acknowledged. As with a previous Jackpine Press book, *We Saw the Elephant: Overland Diaries from the Lander Trail,* working with Karyn has been a pleasure. Jonathan Mayer's illustrations on pages 38, 44,

159, and 188, originally prepared for the Store Per film, appear here with his permission. Special thanks to the two artists for bringing Per to life.

Attributions for the quotations at the heads of chapters are: 1. An adage from Aust-Agder, Norway; 2. Norwegian proverb; 3. Edvard Grieg; 4. Anonymous; 5. *Democratic Review*, June, 1852; 6. Tarald J. Uppstad, Translated by Gunnestein Rystad; 7. Genesis 6:4 (King James Version); 8. Thomas Haynes Bayly; 9. Henrik Ibsen; 10. Anonymous. Nathan Harstad selected the quotations for chapters 2-9. I thank him.

Chapter 1: Birth and Heritage

p. 3   Here and throughout this book (but not always cited in notes), information about Sveio farms and the people who inhabited them is drawn from a *bygedebok* (local history), Simon Steinsbo, *Gards- og aettesoge for Sveio, Band II, Skulekrinsane Bua, Vikse, Vandaskogg og Sveio*, ISBN 82 7096-173-6 (Sveio Kommune, 1987). Catherine Bue brought this source to my attention. See particularly the entries for: Tjernagel, nordre, pp. 99-105; Tjernagelsholmen, pp. 106-112; Tjernagel, sore, pp. 113-119; and Lio (Lien), pp. 340-343. Kari Bergeson, Erling Teigen, and Liv Zemple provided English translations.

pp. 5-6   Material about the birthing process is drawn from Kathleen Stokker, *Remedies and Rituals: Folk Medicine in Norway and the New Land* (Minnesota Historical Society Press, St. Paul, MN, 2007), pp. 38-39, 89, and 14.

p. 6   Peder's baptism and the affirmation of same are documented in International Genealogical Index v 5.0, Norway, Batch No: C428962, 1823-1850, Source Call No.: 0124503 and Finnas *kirkebok* 5 (1823-35), folio 16. The latter lists "Niklas Knutsen Lio, Ola Johannesen Tjernagel, Halldor Johannesen Tjernagel, Kristi Pedersdatter Lio and Brite Jochumsdatter Tjernagel" as sponsors. Terje Gudbrandson of Oslo assisted with these and other records in Norway. PTR has determined that Kjersteen was consistently present at births and baptisms of Peder's siblings and other relatives until her departure for America. Thereafter she assisted at births in Wisconsin, Illinois, and Iowa.

p. 7   Snorre Sturlason, *Heimskringla Or The Lives of the Norse Kings,* Edited with notes by Erling Monsen and translated into English with the assistance of A. H. Smith (D. Appleton and Co., New York, 1932), p. 153.

p. 8 ff.   Moster Church references are scattered through NT's writings. See especially *Walking Trips*, pp. 224-225. Evidence that Moster was, at times, the family's parish church appears in NT's "Dear Folks" letter of July 24, 1892.

"The structure is nearly one thousand years old. I give a description elsewhere, besides which father [Ole Andreas Larson Tjernagel] can tell you all about it seeing he was confirmed there." Pictures of the ancient church as well as architectural and historical details are in *Moster Kirke* (SM Grafisk, Bergen, 1994). Torjus Nordboe provided a copy. PTH visited Moster Church July 21, 2010, with historian Willy Mjanes as guide.

p. 9 ff.   Brother Mark O. Harstad and cousin James P. Olsen, both clergymen, provided insights into theological matters and the history of Lutheranism. An English translation of the Bugenhagen liturgy, along with its music, appears as "The Divine Service, Rite One" in the *Evangelical Lutheran Hymnary* (Morning Star Music Publishers, Inc., St. Louis, Mo, 1996), pp. 41-59.

p. 11   PTH examined the basin July 21, 2010. A photograph of it and a translation of the inscription appear in the *Moster Kirke* booklet.

p. 11-12   On p. 4 Stokker asserts: "A decline in mortality sparked by the introduction of a potato crop and vaccination against smallpox doubled [Norway's] . . . population between 1815 and 1865," resulting in increased impoverishment. She elaborates upon the influence of the "potato pastors" and Dr. Jenner on p. 62. The quotation about pietism is from Bo Giertz, *The Hammer of God, Revised Edition* (Augsburg Books, Minneapolis, MN, 2005), p. 102.

p. 15   *Bygdebok* entries for the Tjernagel farms pin down ownership and *klostergod* details. As follow-up to a July 21, 2010, visit to the Lyse Monastery, historian Willy Mjanes quoted Karl Gervin: "The monasteries of the Cistercians on a rather regular basis developed into big landowners with a broad range of businesses." Gervin labeled them "the first multinational corporations."

p. 17   The characterization of Peer Gynt is from *Minnesota Orchestra Showcase* (Arts & Custom Publishing Co., Inc., Wayzata, MN), Vol. 29, No. 7, March 2007, pp. 39 and 41.

Chapter 2: An Old Country Youth

p. 20-22   NT described the family home at Tjernagel North in *Walking Trips*, pp. 215-216. The description of scenery draws upon Ch. 19 of *Walking Trips,* NT's letter of July 16, 1892, to "Dear Folks at Home," and his letter of August 22, 1910 to PGT. He wrote about the soil at Tjernagel in an extension of the latter dated August 28, 1910.

p. 23   NT recorded the peddler's chant on p. 258 of *Walking Trips.*

p. 24 The quote about homespun is in *Walking Trips*, p. 211. Tools for making wooden shoes are in the possession of cousin John Tjernagel of Marinette, WI.

p. 25 The fresh fish reference appears on p. 96 of *Walking Trips*.

p. 26 PTH inherited such a box, dating from the 1850s.

pp. 27-28 NT wrote his sister Bertha about Aurora Borealis September 24, 1892.

p. 28 Regarding trolls, see NT, *Walking Trips*, pp. 225-226. The Minneapolis *StarTribune*, Sunday August 14, 2005, p. G 1, quoted a report of the Icelandic Tourism Board that 90% of the citizens of that country "take fairies, elves, trolls and other manifestations of huldufolk—'hidden people'—quite seriously," and that the Reykjavik planning department consults with a woman who claims to communicate with them.

p. 29 Hiarnagli is explained in PTR's memo to PTH of November 21, 2006, based on information in the Peter Enwall Collection.

p. 30 Dr. Susan Lederer explained the analemma in a memo of March 1, 2007.

p. 31 The "black eye" quote is from NT, *Contributions to Church Periodicals*, p. 13.

p. 32 The "panorama" reference is in NT's November 15, 1892, letter to PGT.

p. 33 The Rev. Kolbein Espeset to the Rev. Bernard J. Schey, August 19, 1995, and subsequent letters from Espeset to PTH.

p. 34 Terje Gudbrandson located Peder's confirmation record in Finnas *kirkebok* 6 (1836-50), folio 190 B.

Chapter 3: Becoming an Adult

p. 35 NT explained styles of singing in his biography of Nils Peterson in *Passing of the Prairie by a Fossil*, p. 110.

pp. 35-36 The quotations are from Paul W. Heimel, *Oleana: The Ole Bull Colony* (Knox Books, Coudersport, PA, 2002), p. 30.

p. 37 NT wrote about the wedding to "Dear Folks" July 24, 1892.

p. 37-38 Evidence that Store Per and his siblings shared their musical talents at Moster Church is in NT, *Contributions to Church Periodicals,* pp. 139-140.

pp. 39-40 Details about Tjernagelsholmen are from the *bygdebok* entry about the island. The Valborg gang (*Valborglaget*) episode is documented on p. 341 of the Lio (Lien) entry. Mildrid Nickson first brought to my attention the reference to Store Per's son with Johanne on p. 342 of the latter source. PTR to PTH April 15, 2006; Helga Kallevik to PTH February 25, 2007.

p. 41 The quote about the nature of the sea is from NT, *Passing of the Prairie by a Fossil,* Christian Logan, p. 78. Herald Hamre, "Baltic Herring Trade in the Nineteenth Century," at the Stavanger Maritime Museum website.

p. 42 A biography of Jokum in Frank A. Flower, *History of Milwaukee, Wisconsin* (Chicago, 1881), p. 1317 indicates that, before he came to America, Jokum "followed the seas, mostly the Baltic."

pp. 42 ff. NT's biography of "Endre Christenson and Others" in *Passing of the Prairie by a Fossil* is the best (and nearly the only) source about Endre and Store Per's years at sea. The quotations are from pp. 43-45.

p. 45 NT's comments about Ole Andreas' Baltic voyages are in *Contributions to Church Periodicals,* p. 139.

p. 46 Regarding sailors and tobacco see NT, *Walking Trips,* p. 124.

p. 47 Ole Andreas' three-year voyage is documented in LJT's January 8, 1921, letter to Orville G. Wallen. Copy supplied by PTR. NT related the herring and whale episode in *Walking Trips,* pp. 222-224.

pp. 48-49 Insights into North Sea commercial fishing, including the quotation, are from *Walking Trips,* pp. 213-214. The "supply and demand" and "death-toll" quotations are from p. 209 of this source.

p. 50 According to Berit Hanson, "A Life's Work," in *Viking,* August 2006, Vol. 103, No. 8, pp. 16-19, "Iceland and Norway are the only countries that still adhere to the stipulations of Odelsloven."

p. 51-52 The quotation about attractions of America is from NT, *Walking Trips,* p. 92.

Chapter 4: Marriage and Voyage to America

pp. 53-55 Rasmus B. Anderson quoted the article describing the "Sloopers" in *The First Chapter of Norwegian Immigration* (Madison, WI, 1906), pp. 70-71.

Quotes about Peerson, the West, and "America letters" are on pp. 172, 82, and 147.

p. 55 The *Oleana* musical score is in Theodore C. Blegen, et al., *Norwegian Emigrant Songs and Ballads* (University of Minnesota Press, Minneapolis, MN, 1936), p. 194. The humor it generated is documented on p. 187. Blegen's "The Ballad of Oleana: A Verse Translation" is in *Norwegian-American Studies and Records* Vol. 14 (Northfield, MN, 1944), pp. 117-121.

p. 56 LJT wrote to Orville G. Wallen January 18, 1921, about the character of Peder Christenson. The quotation is from a copy of the letter supplied by PTR who also furnished copies of the *Favoriten* and *Therese* ship registers. NT likely made a mistake about the 1852 residence of Peder Christenson in NT, "A leaf from the early life of Endre Christenson Tjernagel; including, also, matter from the life of Peder Larson Tjernagel," a series of articles in *The Story City Herald, September* 28, October 5, 12, 19, and 26, 1922, especially the October 19 segment (cited hereafter as NT, *Herald*, October 19, 1922). This material is similar to NT's "Endre Christenson and Others" in *Passing of the Prairie by a Fossil*, pp. 41-57.

p. 59 The two marriages are recorded in Finnas *kirkebok* 7 (1852-62), folio 208 B; International Genealogical Index v5.0, Norway, Batch No.: M428963, Source Call No.: 0278055.

pp. 61-62 The account of the presumed feast is based on NT, *Walking Trips,* pp. 218-219, NT's November 15, 1892, letter to his sister Bertha, and a miscellany of sources about Norwegian weddings of the period.

p. 62 Terje Gudbrandson located the departure records for these nine in the Finnas Parish register 7 (1852-62), folio 322 A, April 13, 1852.

p. 63 ff. Theodore C. Blegen, *Norwegian Migration to America: The American Transition* (Northfield, MN, 1940), pp. 6-25 is the source for the quotations and generalizations about the Atlantic crossing in this chapter that are not otherwise attributed, including preparations, ship descriptions, loading, sanitation, seasickness, statistics, life at sea, cod fishing, and docking.

p. 65 The quote about schooners is from Blegen, et al., *Norwegian Emigrant Songs and Ballads*, p. 126. Information about the cost of passage aboard the *Kong Sverre* is in a 1970 account by E. J. Henryson, pp. 3-4, provided by Don Hill. Fares paid by the Petersons are documented in NT, *Passing of the Prairie by a Fossil*, Nils Peterson, p. 99.

pp. 65-66 Words and music for the ballad *The Schooner Rogaland* are on pp. 127-129 of *Norwegian Emigrant Songs and Ballads*. The passenger list for the

April 21 to June 10, 1852, Atlantic crossing of the *Rogaland* is accessible online and in National Archives Microfilm M237 Passenger lists of Vessels Arriving at New York, NY, 1820-1897, Roll # 114.

p. 69 Stokker's section on brennevin, "the universal cure," is on *pp.* 194-197 of *Remedies and Rituals.*

pp. 70-71 PGT's account of the Atlantic crossing and the trip inland is in "The Three Kjersteens," an eighteen-page typewritten pamphlet transcribed by Carolyn Teigen Fasel in 1982 from a handwritten manuscript copy of a potential historical article PGT mailed to his brother, HMT, December 20, 1931. Quotations about music aboard ship are on p. 5.

pp. 71-72 Material on the *Aegir, Syttende Mai,* and Ole Rynning is in Blegen et al, *Norwegian Emigrant Songs and Ballads,* p. 24 and ff.

Chapter 5: Transition to Life in America

p. 76 George T. Flom stressed the importance of understanding English in *A History of Norwegian Immigration to the United Sates* (Privately Printed, Iowa City, IA, 1909), p. 26.

pp. 77 ff. Sources for the trip from New York City to Wisconsin are: NT, *Herald,* October 19, 1922; NT, *Passing of the Prairie by a Fossil,* Endre Christenson and Others, pp. 51-53; PGT, "The Three Kjersteens;" and LJT April 10, 1941, untitled, typed, three-page account with an accompanying colored, picture postcard-sized copy of a painting by Emil Biorn (1864-1935). LJT prepared this account in his capacity as "Secretary of the Tjernagel Family Association." Original mailing loaned by Dale Berven. Reference to the possibility that a Norwegian "sailship co." booked the party all the way from Stavanger to Waupaca is in the second paragraph. Biorn's original painting was likely destroyed in a fire at Follinglo Farm December 9, 1968. LJT, PGT, NT, and HMT had opportunities for interviewing people who made the trip or parts of it. NT acknowledged reliance upon interviews with Endre who lived until July 25, 1922. "Mr. Christenson was a good story-teller," NT recorded in *The Story City Herald,* October 26, 1922. At the close of "The Three Kjersteens" PGT wrote: "I have heard parts of this story told by Endre, Jokum, Knute and Kjersti [Phillops] and [Peter] Martin Philops." The first two were participants. The brothers' accounts date from long after the events they report—in LJT's case, eighty-nine years thereafter. Stories had ample opportunities for growing in the telling and for inaccuracies to creep in before they were written.

pp. 79-80 The Erie Canal quotations are from Edward Channing, *A History of the United States, Vol. V, The Period of Transition, 1815-1848* (The Macmillan

Company, New York, 1921), p. 13, and Dan Elbert Clark, *The West in American History* (Thomas Y. Crowell Company, New York, 1937), p. 198. Many Erie Canal websites exist; http://www.eriecanal.org/images.html is one of the best for images.

p. 81-82 Blegen related the Rev. Ottesen impersonator story in *Norwegian Migration to America*, p. 32.

pp. 82-84 The Parkman quotations are from his "Old Northwest Journal & Pontiac Notes 1844-45" in Mason Wade, ed., *The Journals of Francis Parkman* (2 vols., New York Harper & Brothers Publishers, 1947), 1: pp. 301-302 and accompanying notes. Knut Knudsen is quoted in Blegen, et al, *Norwegian Emigrant Songs and Ballads*, pp. 32-33.

The following online source proved useful on the subject of Great Lakes ships and shipping: Patrick Labadie, Brina J. Agranat, and Scott Anfinson, *History and Development of Great Lakes Water Craft* (Minnesota Historical Society, 1997), especially pp. 3-8. For the collision and sinking of the *Atlantic*, see the 1852 online entry of *Annals of Detroit*.

pp. 86 ff. John Tjernagel, Kenneth Lederer, Julie A. Hintz, Clarence A. Chicks, and Roger L. Nichols provided insights into geography in the vicinity of Waupaca and Indians inhabiting that area in 1852. Regarding *Indi-landet* see Richard J. Fapso, *Norwegians in Wisconsin* (The Wisconsin Historical Society Press, Madison, 2001), p. 13 ff. In a letter of February 21, 1990, to Noma Bakros (scanned and shared by PTR), genealogist Gerhard B. Naeseth established that Michael and Anna Marie Lie were living at Koshkonong when their second daughter, Julia Kjerstine, was born December 23, 1850. Between that date and summer 1852 they moved to the vicinity of Waupaca.

pp. 90-91 Jeff Siemers, "From Generation to Generation: The Story of the Stockbridge Bible," a reprint from *The Book Collector*, Vol. 56, No. 1, Spring 2007, loaned by John Tjernagel. The quote is from the last page of the unpaginated text. Chapters 3 and 8 of Patty Loew, *Indian Nations of Wisconsin* (Wisconsin Historical Society Press, Madison, WI, 2001) summarize the histories, respectively, of the Menominee and "Mohican Nation Stockbridge-Munsee Band and Brothertown Indians."

p. 92 Director Julie A. Hintz of the Waupaca Historical Society explained, in a letter of January 24, 2007, that settlers in the vicinity of Waupaca "were squatters on Indian land until the treaty of 1852."

p. 97 Jokum Christenson's citizenship records extracted from the Peter Enwall Collection by PTR. NT's September 8, 1892, letter to his father relates that Jokum's former employee owned the hotel.

p. 98 According to the Wisconsin Bureau of Vital Statistics, "Carl M. Johnson" outlived his wife and at age 86 was "found dead in his room beside his stove while undressing" December 5, 1911. The death certificate lists his occupation as "cooper."

p. 98 Entry for "Canute Phillops" in *Biographical Record and Portrait Album of Webster and Hamilton Counties, Iowa* (Lewis Publishing Co., Chicago, IL, 1889), p. 371.

p. 99 Fredrika Bremer, *The Homes of the New World; Impressions of America, Translated by Mary Howitt*, (2 volumes, Harper & Brothers, New York, 1853), 1: p. 602.

p. 100 Peder Christenson's farms are documented in PTR's April 13, 2006, memo to PTH and accompanying map.

pp. 100 ff. Facts about Store Per and his brother Ole Andreas in Illinois are in *Across the Prairie from Illinois to Iowa 1864. The Story Told by Ole Andreas Larson Tjernagel, Translated by Nehemias Tjernagel*, 28-page mimeographed booklet made by Adolph M. Harstad, September 1976, pp. 14-15. Hereafter cited as *Across the Prairie*. Elmer Baldwin, *The History of La Salle County Illinois* (Rand, McNally & Co., Chicago, 1877) provides context. Pp. 130-134 indicate how residents understood and used the federal land laws. When the Norwegians left Illinois for Iowa they brought with them what they had learned about acquiring land from the United States government. Peder Larson Tjernagel's name does not appear in the 1858 LaSalle County Directory; he was already in Iowa.

p. 103 The quotation about land values is from the previously cited E. J. Henryson account, p. 5.

p. 104-105 Richard Williams and James P. Olsen provided insights about oxen. Olsen proposes an alternate interpretation of the Norwegian word *rosete*. It may be a colloquial variation of *rose,* meaning noble or praiseworthy. If this is the correct reading of *svart rosete*, Buck and Pride were black and distinguished.

p. 104-105 NT, Passing of the Prairie, p. 103.

Chapter 6: An Eye to Iowa

p. 107 Giertz, p. 105. Rev. B. Harstad, *Pioneer Days and other events briefly sketched for the 75th Anniversary of The Synod for the Norwegian Evang. Lutheran Church of America* (Bethany College, Mankato, MN, June, 1928), p. 9.

pp. 108-109 Philip E. Hammond documents disorganization in the Fox River Settlement in "The Migrating Sect: An Illustration from Early Norwegian Immigration" in *Social Forces*, Vol. 41, No. 3, (March 1963), pp. 275-283, brought to my attention by PTR. The quotations are from p. 276.

p. 109 Biographical information on Elling Eielsen and Peter Andreas Rasmusson is scattered through the pages of Olaf Morgan Norlie, *History of the Norwegian People in America* (Augsburg Publishing House, Minneapolis, MN, 1925).

p. 110 B. Harstad, *Pioneer Days*, pp. 25-26.

p. 111 The "dumping ground" quotation is from *Ibid*.

p. 112 Arlen Twedt, Don Hill, Steve Sheldahl, PTR, and PTH have searched a tangle of sources to distinguish between the two Lars Hendersons and to verify that *Taalige* Lars moved his family to the United States in March 1856.

p. 114 ff. All Travaas quotations are from a seventeen-page document "A Little About the First Settlers in Story County by Erik Arnesen Travaas, 1888," translated from Norwegian by Ardis Petersen and Arlen Twedt. Copy generously provided by Arlen and used here with permission. See especially pp. 5-8. The Norwegian version, "Litt om De Forste Settlere i Story County," is in Erik Arnesen Travaas, *Hjemve: Norske Digte og Fortaellinger* (Minneapolis, MN, 1925).

p. 114 NT presented insights into the life and personality of "Lars Henderson (Oiro)" (1825-1908), commonly known as *Taalige* Lars, in *Passing of the Prairie by a Fossil*, pp. 178-180. Identifying him with the place he came from was NT's way of distinguishing him from Lars Henderson (Etne) (1822-1896) who sometimes used the name Henryson and sometimes identified himself with a farm or farms in the vicinity of Etne, Norway, known as Ostebo or Kallestadbakken. Even the descendants of these two men have confused their identities. Lars from Etne had a twin brother, Torkel, who used the name Henryson consistently. LJT prepared an informative biography of *Taalige* Lars Henderson and mailed it to Paul A. Olson, editor of *The Story City Herald*, September 16, 1943. Copy provided by David Henderson.

p. 115 Bliss Perry, ed., *The Heart of Emerson's Journals*, (Houghton Mifflin & Co., Boston, MA, 1926), p. 271.

p. 115 Capt. Marryat, C. B, *Diary in America* (New York, D. Appleton & Co., 1839), p. 124.

p. 116 For Jon Gjerde's articulation of the economic and social aspects of this interpretation see the last citation in the notes for this book. Quotations in the text and below are from p. 233. Gjerde observed a "deep-seated conservative Haugean pietism" coexisting with "novel adaptations in work and leisure" among peasants who made the transition from Balestrand, Norway, to the Upper Middle West. "Whereas the American environment encouraged . . . the maintenance of certain peasant practices, it promoted change in others."

pp. 117-118 NT, *Passing of the Prairie by a Fossil*, "The Sowers Family," pp. 156-157.

p. 119 The "objectionable liquid" quote is from *A Family Album – Story City, Iowa* (Story City, 1975). Pages not numbered.

p. 120 J. W. Lee, *History of Hamilton County, Iowa* (2 vols., J. S. Clarke Publishing Co., Chicago, IL, 1912), 1: pp. 320-321.

p. 120 A May 14, 2007 trip with Mark E. Maggio to a flow near the crest of *Springa Hauen* (Spring Hill), visible from Store Per's farm, brought back memories of an artesian well at nearby Follinglo Farm. As a boy, I deemed such phenomena miraculous. An artesian well still flows on the Jeff Satre farm at the base of *Springa Hauen*.

p. 121 Arlen Twedt furnished a transcription of the Saevereid letter. This is the family of news commentator Eric Sevareid.

p. 122 Ole Andreas' preparations for his trip to Iowa are detailed in *Across the Prairie*, pp. 2, 3, and 17. The technical references are to the wagon's wheel and axle assemblies.

p. 122 Ivar Havneros, "Mindeblad: History of St. Petri Congregation from its foundation in June 1857 to its 50th Jubilee, June 1907," translated by Rachel Vangness, unpublished 29-page document. Arlen Twedt kindly supplied a copy that he has transcribed and annotated. On p. 5 Havneros lists sixteen families in the 1857 migration from Lisbon, Illinois, to the vicinity of Story City: (1) Osmund Henryson and wife, Anna; (2) Samuel Haaland and family; (3) Knud Igland and family; (4) John Charlson Hagen and family; (5) Elling Breiland and family; (6) John Bjorkja and family; (7) Anders Christensen and family; (8) Peder Lars [sic] Tjernagel and family; (9)

Knud Helvig and family; (10) Ole Ritland and family; (11) Lars Henricksen and family; (12) Sivert Mehtvedt and family; (13) Halvor Opstvedt and family; (14) Lars Bouge and family; (15) Knud Aske and family; and (16) Ole T. Hegland family. Numbering and punctuation added by PTH. The spelling is Havneros's, as transcribed by Twedt who has determined that family (15) came to Iowa in 1860. (11) is the *Taalige* Lars Henderson family.

p. 122 Virtues of Buck and Pride are extolled in NT, Passing of the Prairie, p. 103, and in *Across the Prairie*, p. 2.

p. 123 Quotes about the Norwegian trunks and contents are from Travaas, pp. 6-8.

pp. 123-124 NT, *Passing of the Prairie by a Fossil*, Rasmus Sheldall, p. 140 tells of making butter on the road.

pp. 124 E. J. Henryson detailed troubles during the 1856 trek to Iowa on p. 5 of his 1970 account. NT related the "cow overboard" story in Passing of the Prairie, p. 11 and also in *Passing of the Prairie by a Fossil*, Endre Christenson, and Others, p. 46. The quotations are from the former.

p. 125 "Oral History From Clara Malinda Espe" collected by Pat Hosmer "over a period of time in the 1970s." This two-page, typed document is in the possession of Leon Espe. PTR provided a copy.

Chapter 7: A Prairie Home

p. 127 Lee, *History of Hamilton County*, 1: pp. 320-321.

pp. 128-129 Major Wm. Williams, *The History of Early Fort Dodge and Webster County Iowa*, edited by Edward Breen (Messenger Printing Co., Fort Dodge, IA, 1972), pp. 43-45.

pp. 129 ff. Store Per's land holdings are documented in early records in the Hamilton and Story County Courthouses. Tim Neuroth and the staff of Security Title & Abstract, Inc. at Webster City ferreted out pertinent sources in the Hamilton County Courthouse and mailed them to me April 26, 2007. These documents led to "paper chases" in the two courthouses. The latter holds documents pertinent to the property rights of Store Per's daughter, Bertha, a minor at the time of her father's death in 1863. Her guardian filed reports until 1878, many of which Judicial Clerk Dorian Myhre located and copied. Story County Recorder Susan L. Vande Kamp patiently responded to my questions. Cousin Sigrid Hanson located additional reports and the July 19, 1865, appraisal of Peder's estate quoted in Chapter 10. These sources pin down many specifics. I digested them, tramped sections thirty-three and thirty-one, and talked with researchers and lawyers. I then went to the Hamilton County Courthouse September 21, 2007, where Lori Kloberdanz of the Auditor's Office and Assistant Recorder Cheryl Weber helped me. Page 17 of Transfer Book, C. dates "Alpha G. Persons'" land patent in section thirty-three. The text of the patent is on pp. 517-518 of Patent Record Book No. 45, not recorded until May 2, 1908.

Kenneth D. Janssen's February 1982, plat "for Walter and Beverly Mortvedt and for the Riverside Lutheran Bible Camp Association" in the Webster County Auditor's Office is a record of the woodlots in section thirty-one. The plat may be used with inventories and legal descriptions of property Store Per once owned as recorded in his estate files. He bought and sold a number of small parcels.

On May 14, 2007, David McDermott, administrator of the Riverside Lutheran Bible Camp, 3001 Riverside Road, Story City, guided a film crew and me to Store Per's woodlot in section 31. At one time Per also owned additional land in the Skunk River woods. The $520 in "Money an Intrest" listed in the July 19, 1865, inventory likely came from the sale of woodlots either before Per's death or prior to the drafting of the inventory. Five-and-a half acres of "Temer Land" remained in the estate on the date of the inventory.

A February 4, 2008, mailing from Assistant Recorder Cheryl Weber contains documentation from Hamilton County Land Deed Book 2, p. 144 which pins down Lars Henderson's purchase of fifty-three-and one-third acres bordering Store Per's farm on the east. He acquired this land from Alpha G. Person October 6, 1858. An abstract of title furnished by Don Hill shows that Person claimed forty acres of this property as of April 17, 1856. This would have prevented Lars from squatting on these acres in spring 1857 without coming to terms with Person.

p. 130 PTR found Alpha G. Person in the 1856 and 1860 censuses and shared copies of these entries.

p. 132 ff. In 1995 Mark E. Maggio acquired the farmstead in section thirty-three that Store Per once owned. He provided a description of his land, buildings, and operations in a six-page letter of October 12, 2006. The quotation is from p. 3. Dr. Maggio, a sociologist, hosted me at the farm May 13-15, 2007, and again July 13, 2007. I slept in a "four poster" in Malene and Knut Phillops' bedroom and, along with a filming crew, experienced Iowa hospitality at its best. I familiarized myself with the property and discussed details with Dr. Maggio. While restoring the farmhouse he found a carpenter's signature dated 1874 that has led him to conclude that the house was built in that year, four years earlier than reported in *Biographical Record and Portrait Album of Webster and Hamilton Counties, Iowa*, p. 371.

p. 134 Richard and Kay Munson of Story City own the "Anfenson place" and protect its historical integrity.

p. 136 Travaas tells of "kneaded soil" on p. 8;. PGT reported Store Per's efficiency in constructing his cabin in "The Three Kjersteens," p. 13.

p. 136 NT related many specifics of pioneer life in his writings. See especially p. 100 and following of his biographical sketch of Nils Peterson in *Passing of the Prairie by a Fossil*.

p. 136-137 On the economic and political state of affairs in Iowa during the late 1850s see Hubert H. Wubben, *Civil War Iowa and the Copperhead Movement* (Iowa State University Press, Ames, IA, 1980), Ch. 1 and Edgar R. Harlan, *A Narrative History of the People of Iowa* (5 volumes, New York, 1931), 1: Ch. 21. The quotations are from pp. 388 and 385 respectively of the latter. On p. 390 Harlan concluded: "The year 1858 was one of the darkest in Iowa history." Governor Lowe added (p. 391) that the year "was visited with heavy and continuous rains, which reduced the measure of our field crops below one-half the usual products."

p. 137 The February 17, 1857, issue of *The Story County Advocate* reported the protest meeting.

p. 137 Regarding Ole Andreas' first outbuilding see PGT, *The Follinglo Dog Book: A Norwegian Pioneer Story from Iowa* (University of Iowa Press, Iowa City, IA, 1999), pp. 13-14.

pp. 139-140 Bremer, 1: pp. 643-644.

p. 140 E. J. Henryson account, p. 6; NT, *Passing of the Prairie by a Fossil*, p. 177; *ibid.*, p. 144.

p. 143 The "plant-root network," fields, and fences quotations are from NT, *Passing of the Prairie*, pp. 45-47.

pp. 143-144 Nathan H. Parker, *The Iowa Handbook, For 1857. With a New and Correct Map* (John P. Jewett, Boston, MA, 1857), pp. 12-13.

pp. 144-145 Regarding malaria in central Iowa see NT, *Passing of the Prairie by a Fossil*, Hans B. Henryson, pp. 68, 74. PTH quoted Holverson in "Disease and Sickness on the Wisconsin Frontier: Malaria," in *Wisconsin Magazine of History*, Vol. 43, No. 2, (Winter, 1959-60), p. 96. Scientists later discovered that female anopheles mosquitoes carry the malaria parasite and that plowing and draining destroy the carrier's breeding places. Studies prove that anopheles mosquitoes would rather feed on cattle than humans. Consequently, with the rise of dairy herds, the introduction of window screens, and the lowering of the water table, malaria diminished and eventually disappeared from Iowa and the Midwest.

p. 145 Regarding water and wells see NT, Passing of the Prairie, pp. 70-74. "Pump Lars" appears in PGT and HMT, "Who Was Nagelsen," in *The Palimpsest*, Vol. 13, No. 7, July 1932, p. 262.

p. 145 Travaas reported continuing migration of people to the Story City area from Illinois and Norway, pp. 8-9.

pp. 146-147 NT tells the "Walter" story in Passing of the Prairie, pp. 185-186. It appears in nearly identical form in *Passing of the Prairie by a Fossil*, Endre Christenson and Others, pp. 47-48; it also appears in PGT's *Follinglo Dog Book*, p. 19.

Chapter 8: Stories from the Prairie

p. 149 PGT, *Follinglo Dog Book*, p. 19. PGT and his siblings communicated with Ole Andreas (their father), Endre Christenson, Jokum Christenson, and others who knew Store Per and witnessed his feats. Ole lived until 1919 and Endre until 1922. Ole's sons wrote similar versions of the same stories.

pp. 149-152 NT wrote about the 1859 visit in *Passing of the Prairie by a Fossil*, Christian Logan, pp. 80-81. Logan was not his name until the Civil War when he ceased using the name Christenson and took the name of a soldier he admired. Quotations from and about the visit also appear in: Obituary of Ole Andreas Larson Tjernagel in *Visergutten*, May 22, 1919, translated from Norwegian by Adolph M. Harstad in 1976, p. 1; NT, Passing of the Prairie, pp. 9-11; and in NT, *Passing of the Prairie by a Fossil*, Endre Christenson, and Others, p. 47.

p. 152 W. O. Payne, *History of Story County, Iowa: A Record of Settlement, Organization, Progress and Achievement* (2 vols., The S. J. Clarke Publishing Co., Chicago, IL, 1911), 1: p. 112. During a conversation of June 24, 2006, at PTH's home in Lakeville, MN, Bertha Tjernagel, daughter of HMT, recounted stories that came down to her about Store Per's sensitivity to children.

pp. 152-153 The snake story is from PGT, *Follinglo Dog Book*, pp. 94-95.

pp. 153-155 Regarding the mired cow see: NT, Passing of the Prairie, p. 187; PGT, *Follinglo Dog Book,* p. 22; and NT, *Passing of the Prairie by a Fossil,* Endre Christenson, and Others, pp. 49-50.

p. 155 NT, *Herald,* October 12, 1922.

pp. 155-157 The Egland stories are found in PGT, "The Three Kjersteens," p.13; *Across the Prairie,* p. 8; and in NT, *Passing of the Prairie by a Fossil,* Pioneer Pictures, p. 192.

pp. 157-158 The near drowning of Buck and Pride is related in NT, *Passing of the Prairie by a Fossil,* Endre Christensen and Others, p. 46, and in PGT, *Follinglo Dog Book,* pp. 37-38.

p. 160-161 The flourmill story is in PGT, *Follinglo Dog Book,* p. 20 and in NT, *Passing of the Prairie by a Fossil,* Endre Christensen and Others, p. 48.

p. 161-162 The sawmill story is in PGT, *Follinglo Dog Book,* pp. 20-21 where the name is spelled "Linsey," and in NT Passing of the Prairie, p. 91 and *Passing of the Prairie by a Fossil,* Endre Christensen and Others, pp. 48-49 where it is spelled "Lindsey."

pp. 162-164 The quote about Per's temper is in *ibid,* pp. 44-45; that about driftwood is on p. 45.

p. 164-165 The "I've got it" story is from PGT, *Follinglo Dog Book,* p. 21; NT's version is in Passing of the Prairie, p. 188.

pp. 165-166 NT, *Passing of the Prairie by a Fossil,* Michael Hegland, p. 66.

p. 167 The soil survey is quoted in NT, *Historical Sketch . . . The Sheldall School,* (no place or date of publication indicated), p. 7.

pp. 169-170 Regarding winter in Iowa, see NT, *Passing of the Prairie by a Fossil,* Nils Anderson, p. 18. James Sowers thought skiing "the oddest means of locomotion imaginable," *ibid,* The Sowers Family, p. 158.

p. 170 The aromas quote is in NT, Passing of the Prairie, p. 86.

Chapter 9: A School, a War, Some Indians, and a Church

p. 171 NT, *Sheldall School,* p. 7; NT, *Passing of the Prairie by a Fossil,* Nils Peterson, p. 100.

p. 172 NT, *Sheldall School,* p. 11.

ACKNOWLEDGEMENTS, SOURCES, AND NOTES

pp. 172-173 Sketch of Captain W. A. Wier in *Story City* (1975), not paginated; NT, *Passing of the Prairie by a Fossil*, William A. Wier, p. 171.

pp. 173-174 Bremer, 2: p. 434.

p. 174 United States citizenship certificate of "Ole A. Larson," April 21, 1868. Copy in possession of PTH. At this time, Ole was not using Tjernagel as part of his name. He did so after his sons used it to distinguish themselves from other Larsons in the Story City area.

pp. 174-175 Robert W. Johannsen, Editor, *The Lincoln-Douglas Debates of 1858* (Oxford University Press, NY, 1965), especially Ch. 3.

pp. 175-176 PGT, "Erik Kjyten, Our First Tinner, Watch Maker and Barber," in *Story City Herald*, February 13, 1930.

p. 176 Arlen Twedt shared a draft of his forthcoming essay, "Osmund Sheldahl, Pastor and Pathfinder," which explains Sheldahl's early orientation toward the Republican Party. *Emigranten* was published at Inmansville, WI, 1852-1857 and at Madison, WI, 1857-1868.

p. 176 Odd S. Lovoll, *The Promise of America; A History of the Norwegian-American People* (University of Minnesota Press, Minneapolis, MN, 1984, in cooperation with The Norwegian-American Historical Association), pp. 71-72 and 75.

p. 177 LJT, "Scott Township History," in *Supplement October 24, 1940, The Story City Herald Anniversary Number*, a 128-page bound book (Story City, IA, 1940), pp. 124-125. Entry for Knute Phillops in *Biographical Record and Portrait Album of Webster and Hamilton Counties, Iowa*, p. 371. His name is spelled many ways in the sources. Service records of the Norwegian-American Civil War soldiers are accessible in an online database maintained by Vesterheim Norwegian-American Museum in Decorah, IA.

pp. 178-179 NT, *Passing of the Prairie by a Fossil*, Christian Logan, p.78.

p. 179 L. G. Bennett and Wm. M. Haigh, *History of the Thirty-Sixth Regiment Illinois Volunteers, During the War of the Rebellion* (Aurora, IL, 1876), pp. 45-46.

p. 179 The proclamation is in Roy P. Basler, Ed., *The Collected Works of Abraham Lincoln* (Rutgers University Press, New Brunswick, NJ, 1953) 6: pp. 203-204.

pp. 179-180 For Lars' Civil War service see NT, *Passing of the Prairie by a Fossil*, Lars Henderson (Oiro), pp. 178-180; *Biographical Record and Portrait Album of Hamilton and Wright Counties, Iowa*, pp. 297-298; and LJT to Paul A.

231

Olson, September 16, 1943. In the later, LJT contended that the confusion over the identities of the two Lars Hendersons was deliberate. *Taalige* Lars, "Through some Hocus-Pocus . . . allowed himself to be drafted into the Civil War, when it was really Lars Henryson Ostebo that was drafted. That is when Lars Henryson Ostebo became Lars Henderson, instead of Lars Henryson." LJT added: "*'Taalige* Lars' was always proud of his war record and he was a loyal G.A.R. man." During the Civil War it was legal for a draftee to pay a substitute to serve in his place.

p. 180 NT, *Passing of the Prairie by a Fossil*, Nils Anderson, p. 19.

pp. 180 ff. Regarding Indians in central Iowa in 1857 and thereafter see: William G. Allen, *A History of Story County, Iowa* (Iowa Printing Co., Des Moines, IA, 1887), pp. 9-10 and 17; NT, *Passing of the Prairie by a Fossil*, Rasmus Sheldall, p. 143 and *ibid.*, Endre Christenson, and Others, pp. 56-57.

pp. 181-182 Julian E. McFarland, *A History of the Pioneer Era on the Iowa Prairies* (Graphic Publishing Co., Lake Mills, IA, 1969), p. 145.

p. 182 Reference to Erik's horse is in PGT, *Follinglo Dog Book*, p. 77; Ole's encounter with Indians is related on p. 8.

p. 182-183 The students' visit to the Indian camp is related in PGT, *Follinglo Dog Book*, pp. 90-91.

p. 184 ff. Entry for Rev. Rasmussen in *Norsk lutherske prester i Amerika, 1843-1913* (Augsburg Publishing House, Minneapolis, MN, 1914), p. 101; Travaas, p. 9; NT, Red Scrapbook at State Historical Society of Iowa at Iowa City, p. 13. Havneros, p. 7. Microfilm copies of many St. Petri records are in the Bertha Bartlett Public Library in Story City, the earliest of them in the Norwegian language. Record series are not clearly identified and parts of the film are out of focus and difficult to read.

p. 185 The baptism quote is from NT, *Passing of the Prairie by a Fossil*, Rasmus Sheldall, p. 144.

pp. 185-186 Entry for Rev. Amlund in *Norsk lutherske prester i Amerika*, p. 105. The quote attributed to him is from "St. Petri Lutheran Congregation," in the 1940 *Story City Herald Anniversary Number*, pp. 98-99. No Rasmussen or Amlund papers have been located, but see Norwegian-American Historical Association online where a "Report of the Annual Meeting of the Haugean Churches Held at Lisbon, Illinois, in June, 1854, Translated and edited by J. Magnus Rohne." Reproduced from Vol. IV of that organization's *Studies and Records*. In his introduction Rohne states that Rasmussen "remained outside of all synodical connections until 1862, when, together with the Revered Nils Amlund and the Reverend John W. Field, he joined the Norwegian Synod."

p. 186 NT wrote of the church building in *Passing of the Prairie by a Fossil*, Hans B. Henryson, pp. 74-76.

p. 187 NT, *Sheldall School*, pp. 3-4.

pp. 187-188 NT recorded this version of Wier's account of the salt barrel contest in Passing of the Prairie, p. 186 and a nearly identical version of it in *Passing of the Prairie by a Fossil*, William A. Wier, pp. 171-172.

p. 189 Travaas, p. 11.

Chapter 10: Death of Store Per

p. 191 LJT to Orville G. Wallen, January 8, 1921.

p. 192 The quote about Per and musical tradition is in NT, *Passing of the Prairie by a Fossil*, The Riverside Band, p. 227.

p. 193 ff. Regarding the Norwegian Synod's position on slavery see the Evangelical Lutheran Synod's website. In 1861 the position was: "Although according to the Word of God it is not in itself sin to have slaves, yet slavery is an evil and a punishment from God, and we condemn all the abuses and sins which are connected with it, just as we, when our call requires it and Christian charity and wisdom demand it, will work for its abolition."

p. 193-194 The questions are from Ulrik Vilhelm Koren, "Abraham Lincoln: A Lecture for the Students at Luther College on Lincoln's Birthday, 12 February [1901]," translated from the Norwegian by Mark DeGarmeaux in 2008, p. 126, and used here with his permission. Page numbers refer to a 1901 reprint of the speech in the Norwegian language rather than to the translation. The quote about Koren's members is from p. 90. Koren's quote about "all" Synod pastors being against slavery is in George O. Lillegard, ed., *Faith of Our Fathers* (Lutheran Synod Book Co., Mankato, MN, 1953), p. 104. Further discussion of slavery issues within the Norwegian Synod is in B. Harstad, *Pioneer Days*, pp. 28 ff.

p. 195 Precise documentation for Iowans' support of the Union cause is in Robert R. Dykstra, "Iowa 'Bright Radical Star.'" I used a reprint of this work from James C. Mohr, ed., *Radical Republicans in the North: State Politics during Reconstruction* (The Johns Hopkins University Press, Baltimore, MD, 1976), specifically, Table 2 on p. 172.

p. 196 Koren, *Abraham Lincoln*, p. 130.

p. 196 ff. The author possesses a copy of Bertha's hand written, two-page account of Store Per's death. See also PGT's account in "The Three Kjersteens," pp. 14-15.

pp. 196-197 Reference to LJT's artesian well is from a 1938 newspaper article in his Green Scrapbook on loan to PTH. Titled "Much Water From Small Flow," it likely appeared in *The Story City Herald*.

p. 198 The description of the people is from Travaas, p. 9.

p. 199 In Amlund's absence Pastor Sheldahl served both his own Palestine congregation south of Story City and the St. Petri congregation. He strove to steer a middle course between the liturgical Norwegian Synod and the followers of Hans Nielsen Hauge who wanted a simpler, less formal service with lay participation. A biographical entry for Rev. Sheldahl is in *Norsk lutherske prester i Amerika*, p. 105.

p. 199 *Evangelical Lutheran Hymnary*, Hymn # 553. No record of Store Per's death or funeral can be found in the microfilmed records of St. Petri Congregation cited in the previous chapter. The death of "Peder Larson" on "February 28, 1863," and the names of his parents are recorded in LJT's "carefully made copy of the Church Records of St Petri Congregation" in the Tjernagel collection at the State Historical Society of Iowa in Iowa City, but there is no reference to a funeral.

p. 199 Ole Andreas Olson Tjernagel related Lars' reaction to his son's death to me July 5, 1983, at Tjernagel, Norway, with my father, Adolph M. Harstad, serving as translator.

p. 200 Nils Peterson's work on Malene's farm is documented in NT's biography of him in *The Passing of the Prairie by a Fossil*, p. 104.

p. 200 Destiny has not been kind to *Taalege* Lars Henderson. The Grand Army of the Republic marker he deserves adorns Lars Henryson/Henderson's grave in Mt. Olive Cemetery in Roland, Iowa—a prime example of confusion of the identities of these two men.

pp. 201-201 I am grateful to cousin Sigrid Hanson for finding and sharing the appraisal of Store Per's estate in the Story County Courthouse in Nevada.

p. 202 PGT knew his neighbor, Knute Phillops, very well and recorded his decisiveness in "The Three Kjersteens," p. 16. The entry for "Canute

Phillops" in *Biographical Record and Portrait Album of Webster and Hamilton Counties, Iowa*, p. 731 contains errors.

p. 203 PGT grew up with his cousin and schoolmate, Bertha. He recorded the story of her strength in "The Three Kjersteens," p. 15. Her obituary is in *The Story City Herald* November 24, 1932, the same year PGT died.

p. 203-204 Email exchanges with Helga Kallevik, especially her memo of March 4, 2007. Focusing on Peder Pederson proved challenging because the name is common and because he moved from place to place while parish boundaries shifted. Terje Gudbrandson and PTR corroborate Helga's evidence.

p. 204 PGT, "The Three Kjersteens," opening and closing sections.

p. 205 NT's assessment of Store Per appears in *Passing of the Prairie by a Fossil,* Endre Christenson, and Others, p. 11.

Epilogue

p. 207 The Thoreau quotes are from his *A Week on the Concord and Merrimack Rivers*, as found in, and analyzed by Wilson O. Clough in, *The Necessary Earth: Nature and Solitude in American Literature* (University of Texas Press, Austin, TX, 1964), p. 77 ff.

pp. 209-210 Unpaginated 3 x 5¾ inch pamphlet, *Memories Being an Address by A. M. Henderson Given at the Thirty-Fifth Annual Old Settlers Picnic at Bell's Mill, Hamilton Count Ia. Sunday, August 1, 1937.* Copy on loan to PTH. The speaker, an alumnus of Sheldall School, was a son of pioneer Lars Henderson/Henryson (Etne) who built the schoolhouse.

pp. 210-211 Communications from Leon Espe including his two-page "Memories and Stories I Heard."

Two exemplary books for fitting Store Per into larger contexts are: Allan G. Bogue, *From Prairie To Cornbelt: Farming on the Illinois and Iowa Prairies in the Nineteenth Century* (The University of Chicago Press, Chicago, IL, 1963) and Jon Gjerde, *From Peasants to Farmers: The Migration from Balestrad, Norway, to the Upper Middle West* (Cambridge University Press, Cambridge, 1985). Gjerde focuses on cultural patterns and change (including gender roles) in two groups — those who remained on Norway's west coast and those who left for the Midwest in the nineteenth century.

Back Cover

Born in Norway, Emil Biorn (1864-1935) spent his productive years as an artist and musician in Chicago. Two institutions in Decorah, Iowa, hold examples of his works—the Fine Arts Collection of Luther College and Vesterheim Norwegian American Museum. Early in the twentieth century, Nehemias Tjernagel commissioned Biorn, his friend, to produce this work. The original cannot be found and was likely destroyed in a 1968 fire. However, in 1941 members of the Tjernagel Family Association received colored 4 inch by 6 ½ inch photographic copies of it from their energetic secretary, L. J. Tjernagel. Dale Berven loaned the copy his father received. Using computer software, Philip T. Rhodes freshened up the colors. Many thanks to Dale and Phil.

INDEX

Many Norwegian-Americans used the name of the farm they came from as part of their names. Some did not; others vacillated. Below, "Tjernagel" appears in parentheses after the names of people from the two farms of that name. Two abbreviations are used: SP for Store Per and aka for "also known as."

emigrants and Indians with
violin, 89-90; climbs agricultural
ladder, 96, 99; in 1855 Illinois
census, 100; scouting trip, 115-
121; 1857 move s to Iowa, 122-
125; establishes farm, 129-138;
Helga dies in prairie fire, 152;
road supervisor, 155; loses
temper, 45, 162-164; in 1860
Iowa census, 167-168; active in
school and church, 171, 184-186;
death and burial, 196-200; estate
inventory, 201
    Strongman stories: blocks path
to church with boulder, 38;
anchor lifting contest, 43-45;
carries "pack mule" load to
Koshkonong, 94; cradles twelve
acres of grain a day, 101;
competes with reaping machine,
102-103; lifts cow from Mississippi, 124; pushes wagons out of
mud, 125; builds cabin in short
time, 136; throws bully at cabin
bee, 146-147; lifts cow from
mire, 153-155; rips out fence
blocking road, 155; saves ox
from drowning and takes its
place in yoke, 157-159; uses
strength and humor at grain
mill, 160-161; foils pranksters at
saw mill, 161-162; prevents
falling beams from injuring
men, 164-166; wins salt barrel
lifting contest, 187-188; calls
bluff of ethnic challenger, 189
    SP's spiritual life: 6, 17, 33-34,
71, 95-96, 107-112, 116, 163-164,
184-186, 189-190, 193-194, 199,
209-210
    Children with Malena listed in
her entry
Lie, Michael, 56-57, 62, 86-94, 97,
121

Lien farm, 3-5, 14-16, 19-20, 31-33,
39, 50, 56, 75, 98, 213
Lincoln, Abraham, 174-175, 177,
179, 191, 193, 195, 196
log cabins, 119-120, 133-136, 138,
141-142, 151
Lyse Monastery, 15, 16

malaria (ague), 72, 144-145, 192
military land warrant, 130
Moster Church, 6-11, 13, 20, 33,
37, 110, 191
music (including violin), 1, 35-38,
61-62, 70-72, 89, 95, 100, 134-135,
173, 186, 192

Norse myths and gods, 5-6, 28-30
Norway Township (aka Scott),
120-121, 127-128, 132-133, 155,
157, 163, 167-168, 171, 173, 186
187, 204
Norwegian Synod, 108, 111, 184-
186, 193-194, 196

Olson, Ole Andreas (Tjernagel),
38, 213
Omundsen, Jon, 6
Ottesen, Rev. Jacob Aal, 81-82

Panic of 1857, 131, 136-137
Parkman, Francis, 82-85
peat, 4-5, 20, 23, 25, 38, 213
Pedersdatter, Helga (Tjernagel,
SP's mother, married to Lars
Johanneson), 3, 5-7, 13-14, 24-25,
29, 33, 37, 42, 60
Pedersdatter, Kjersteen
(Tjernagel, SP's aunt, married to
Phillipus Knutson), 5-7, 13-14,
19, 40, 42, 56, 87, 93-94, 96, 98-
100, 103, 132-133, 150, 202, 204
Pederson, Peder (SP's son by
Johanne), 40-41, 203-204
Peerson, Cleng, 54, 100, 183

ABOUT THE AUTHOR

I read mainstream histories, best sellers about politicians and generals, specialized studies in areas of particular interest, and also books about "We the people." Abraham Lincoln is alleged to have said: "God must love the common man, he made so many of them." Good biographies of common people are had to find. As was the case with the making of his book, the details must be dug out of family collections, church records, courthouses, libraries, and state and local historical societies. Except for the strongman theme, Stor Per's life was ordinary. Details of how ordinary lives intersect with broad themes of history fascinate me.

Historical sleuthing sometimes brings surprises. As I was working on a biography of Iowa Congressman Gilbert N. Haugen during the mid 1970s, my research led to one of his well-worn pocket diaries. Here I found an entry about a young preacher ordained and installed at Richland Lutheran Church, Thornton, Iowa, June 20, 1926. He was my father, the Rev. Adolph M. Harstad! While hammering out legislation to cope with the persistent farm depression of the 1920s, the Congressman, then Chairman of the House Agriculture Committee, came back to his home state to interact with the people. Upon reading his note about meeting my father I realized as never before that national history is linked to the story of my own people.

When properly pursued, we are likely to find that all history is of the same fabric. We are all part of it. We might even debate whether national history is the concentrated history of "We the people."

Peter Tjernagel Harstad earned an AA from Bethany Lutheran College and a BS, MS, and PhD from the University of Wisconsin, Madison, with concentrations in history. He held a Ford Foundation-financed post doctoral fellowship in advanced historical editing at the University of Kentucky. Peter taught at Hoover High School, Flint Michigan; Idaho State University; University of Washington; University of Iowa; and Bethany Lutheran College. He was director of the Iowa and Indiana Historical Societies, where he served from 1972-1981 and 1984-2001 respectively. He retired in 2001. Peter currently lives in Lakeville, MN, where he pursues his favorite activity — historical research and writing.

ABOUT THE ARTIST

In the summer of 2009, Michael and I were fresh out of college, recently married, and in search of a new church home. Following one of our visits to Heritage Lutheran Church in Apple Valley, MN, a man who looked vaguely familiar approached me and asked if I would be interested in an illustration project. And, as the saying goes, "the rest is history."

Of course, the man was Peter Tjernagel Harstad, the author of this book. I soon discovered that he is a first cousin of my grandmother, Amanda (Tjernagel) Madson. Anyone who has ever met my grandmother knows that she is a grand storyteller. This trait must run deep in the Tjernagel blood lines because *Store Per* is an impressive piece of literature. I am proud to claim ties to this family and am honored to have lent an artist's hand to the telling of Per's story.

The particular pen-and-ink style of the *Store Per* illustrations is similar to the effect produced by various printmaking techniques; both result in an image that appears to be scratched or cut into. In contrast to smooth gradients and soft edges, the rough, chiseled appearance of the repetitive pen marks and sharp edges evokes a sense of the toil, earthiness, and sometimes pain so familiar to Store Per, Malena, and their fellow emigrants.

Karyn E. Lukasek received her BA in Studio Art from Bethany Lutheran College, Mankato, MN, in 2009, where she held a four-year Ylvisaker Scholarship. As a student, Karyn received numerous art-related awards and recognitions. Her primary media include pen and ink, oil on canvas, and cut paper collage. She especially enjoys creating material for children and is both author and illustrator of the children's book, *Where Did the World Come From?* (Concordia Publishing House, St. Louis, MO, 2011). Karyn also collaborated with Peter on the artistic production of *We Saw the Elephant: Overland Diaries from the Lander Trail* (Jackpine Press, Lakeville, MN, 2010). She and her husband Michael currently live near the Twin Cities with their son, Isaac.